Preparing to Care

Induction and practice development for residential social workers

Predencia Gabbidon and Barry Goldson

The National Children's Bureau (NCB) works to identify and promote the well-being and interests of all children and young people across every aspect of their lives.

NCB is a registered charity which encourages professionals and policy makers to see the needs of the whole child and emphasises the importance of multidisciplinary, cross-agency partnerships. It has adopted and works within the UN Convention on the Rights of the Child and according to NCB stated values and principles.

It collects and disseminates information about children and promotes good practice in children's services through research, policy and practice development, membership, publications, conferences, training and an extensive library and information service.

Several Councils and Fora are based at NCB and contribute significantly to the breadth of its influence. It also works in partnership with Children in Scotland and Children in Wales and other voluntary organisations concerned for children and their families.

Published by National Children's Bureau Enterprises, the trading company for the National Children's Bureau. Registered Charity number 258825.

ISBN 1 900990 31 8

© National Children's Bureau, 1998
8 Wakley Street, London EC1V 7QE. Tel: 0171 843 6000. www.ncb.org.uk

Printed by Futura, London.

Contents

Appendices 295

Acknowledgements

If it were not for a partnership between the Children's Residential Care Unit at the National Children's Bureau and the Department of Health, the research for and the writing of this book would not have been possible. Furthermore our work has been informed and assisted by consultation with many individuals and agencies to whom we are grateful.

In particular we wish to thank colleagues from Surrey Social Services Department who have piloted the manual within children's homes and whose feedback and critical comment has been invaluable: Louise Erskin, Carol Murphy and Alison Walker from Squirrel Lodge; Sharon Newton, Jan Power and Jocelyn Scott-Boyle from Burbank; and Nigel Bishop, Sandra Hooper and Fiona West from Highfield. We are equally grateful to Gordon Chinchen, Simon Harrison and William Williamson from the social services management team in Surrey.

Isabelle Brodie, Barbara Kahan, John Jerwood and John Rowlands, as readers, offered incisive comments and helpful suggestions which have informed and shaped some of our ideas.

Finally our special thanks go to David Crosbie from the Department of Health and Steve Howell from the National Children's Bureau who have been consistently helpful and to Emma Richards for her unwavering patience in working on an ever-changing manuscript.

Residential care is a complex and demanding endeavour. The children and young people who are looked after in residential homes deserve a responsive and effective service. We hope that this book will make a meaningful contribution to the professional development of residential social workers and enable them through their practice, to meet the individual and collective needs of the children and young people with whom they work.

Predencia Gabbidon and Barry Goldson
1998

Predencia Gabbidon is a Senior Development Officer with the National Children's Bureau.

Barry Goldson is a lecturer at the Department of Sociology, Social Policy and Social Work Studies at the University of Liverpool.

Introduction

Background

As a member of staff in a children's home, you are at the 'forefront of service delivery. Yours is not an easy job, and you are expected to work under difficult circumstances. At times you may find that you are expected to cope with situations that you have not been trained for. You have probably found too few people outside this area of work have any real idea of what the job is about. In good homes staff know what they are trying to do and how they intend to do it.

(SSI, 1994, Briefing Paper 2)

...it is important to note that many children and young people who live or have lived in residential care are able to tell us that they have found it a positive and rewarding experience.

(Kahan, 1994; 26)

The message from these two extracts is clear; residential social work staff must know 'what they are trying to do and how they intend to do it', if children and young people are to be provided with a 'positive and rewarding experience' in residential care.

Preparing to Care is the third of a sequence of National Children's Bureau publications to address explicitly induction and staff development in residential child care. Following the publication of *A Sense of Security* (Goldson, 1995) and *Securing Best Practice* (Gabbidon and Goldson, 1997) *Preparing to Care* provides a comprehensive framework to guide the induction and development of residential social workers.

Who is the manual for?

The manual is designed to be used by residential social work staff in children's homes. It may also be used by other professionals in residential homes including teachers and first line managers.

What is induction?

The objective of the induction process is to assimilate new members of staff into their place of work and to help them become effective as quickly as possible.

Why induction is important

> Employers ought to provide sufficient resources to ensure that a *planned* period of induction can be provided for all staff . . . there needs in all cases to be a structured and systematic process which aims to integrate the new member of staff into the work of the home and into the team of staff whom he or she will work with.
>
> (Warner (1992) *Choosing with Care,* pp.129-30)

Working with children and young people in residential homes can be richly rewarding, providing opportunities to form close and meaningful professional relationships, to offer guidance and assistance to the children and young people and to help them develop their full potential. The work can also be demanding. Many of the children in residential homes have disrupted and unhappy backgrounds. The residential placement provides the stability within which they can develop and progress. The individual and collective needs of the children and young people in residential homes are often complex. You will be able to respond to these needs more effectively if you are introduced to the work in a structured manner which clearly outlines what is expected of you, your colleagues, your supervisor and the children and young people.

The day-to-day practice in residential homes requires you to take full account of the following key issues:

The duty to safeguard and promote the welfare of children
This is the cornerstone of best residential social work with children and young people. Best practice recognises the rights, needs, wishes, feelings and dignity of each child and young person.

The legal status of the child/young person and the plans for their care.
Children and young people enter residential care for different reasons and via different legal routes. You will have opportunites to develop your knowledge in relation to the legal framework throughout your induction.

The age of the child/young person
Residential homes provide accommodation for children and young people of different ages and practice in the homes should reflect this.

The religious persuasion, ethnic origin and cultural and linguistic background of the child/young person.
Residential homes are required by the Children Act 1989 to develop practices which take into account the religious persuasion, ethnic origin and cultural and linguistic background of children and young people.

The relationship of the child/young person with their family
A central objective of best child care is to work in partnership with the families of children and young people who are looked after in residential homes.

2

These key issues will be addressed throughout your induction.

A number of inquiries and reports have established the need for effective induction of staff in residential work with children and young people. These include: Levy and Kahan (1991) *The Pindown Experience and the Protection of Children*; Utting (1991) *Children in the Public Care*; Howe (1992) *The Quality of Care*; Warner (1992) *Choosing with Care*; and Goldson (1995) *A Sense of Security.* Your supervisor or training officer will be able to advise you on how to obtain these. They should be available within your employing department.

Objectives of the manual

The objectives of this manual are:

- to introduce you to the home, its purpose and function and the services it provides for children and young people;

- to introduce you to the policies and practices of the home and your role within it;

- to enable you to understand the important balance between meeting the individual needs of the child/young person and the collective needs of the children and young people in residential care;

- to provide opportunities within which you will develop your skills and become an effective and responsive residential social worker;

- to enable you to use your existing skills and knowledge within the home while offering opportunities for you to acquire and develop new ones;

- to enable you to meet with staff from other agencies and to share and develop an understanding of best child care practice;

- to provide a firm foundation for your future professional development, education and training;

- to help you to understand the contribution of your home within the wider context of children's services provision;

- to provide a structure for your supervision, and to help you and your supervisor to monitor and support your progress in order to facilitate a fair assessment of your practice at the end of your probationary period;

- to help you to establish clear lines of communication and accountability.

Using *Preparing to Care*

Your *Preparing to Care* manual is not a textbook, it is an *open learning tool* which contains a wide variety of exercises and activities that have been designed to help you to develop the values, knowledge and skills that are required of a residential social worker. One of the benefits of this approach to induction is that it enables you to progress at your own pace within your probationary period.

If you already have experience of working in residential homes (particularly with children and young people), you *may* complete *Preparing to Care* more quickly and easily than a colleague who is completely new to residential social work. There is, however, little to be gained by rushing through the manual without reaching an understanding of the principles and values that underpin the exercises.

Completing the modules

There are three modules in the manual.

Module 1 concentrates on your introduction to the staff, children and young people; the purpose and function of the home; and safety procedures in the home. Also in this module are exercises and activities which will enable you to identify important aspects of personnel practice. We recommend that you aim to complete this module within the first **two weeks** in post. The order in which you complete the sections in each of the modules will be agreed between you and your supervisor.

Module 2 focuses more closely on some of the issues introduced in Module 1 and addresses many other practice issues. You should aim to complete this module within the first **four months** of working in the home.

Module 3 is designed to help you to consolidate your knowledge and understanding of the services your home provides within the broader context of child care provision. You should aim to complete this module by the end of your **sixth month** as a residential social worker.

You will need to consult a number of documents in order to complete each module successfully and these are listed in the separate introductions and referenced at the end of each of the modules.

Supervision and evaluation

Your progress will be monitored continuously by your supervisor. At the end of each section in the manual there is an evaluation form for your supervisor to complete as a part of a formal supervision session. Your practice will be assessed using the following learning criteria, which are adapted from Birmingham Polytechnic's *Practice Teacher's Handbook.*

Acquaintance	You are introduced to knowledge/skills. At this stage you are not familiar with them. You require demonstration, explanation and further training/practice.
Familiarity	You are familiar with the knowledge/skills. You can recognise and describe them in others, but cannot yet demonstrate them yourself.
Ability to use	You can recognise and describe the knowledge/skills and can also demonstrate them in your daily work. There are still, however, occasions when you are hesitant and require reminders.
Relative proficiency	You can work independently in carrying out most of your routine tasks but require guidance on values which underpin the tasks.
Competence	The values, knowledge and skills are internalised and are now an integral part of your work.

It may be necessary for some sections to be assessed on more than one occasion in order to record your progress accurately. Where this happens each evaluation should be dated by your supervisor. Any comments should be signed by both you and your supervisor.

Confidentiality

As you complete this manual you should be mindful that it is a confidential document and your agency's policy and practice regarding confidentiality should be observed.

References

Birmingham Polytechnic (1978) *Practice Teacher's Handbook* from original work of Bertha Reynolds, University of Chicago

Gabbidon, P and Goldson, B (1997) *Securing Best Practice: An induction manual for residential staff working in secure accommodation.* National Children's Bureau

Goldson, B (1995) *A Sense of Security: Curricula for the induction and training of staff in secure accommodation.* National Children's Bureau

Howe (1992) *The Quality of Care.* Local Government Management Board

Kahan, B (1994) *Growing up in Groups.* HMSO

Levy, A and Kahan, B (1991) *The Pindown Experience and the Protection of Children.* Staffordshire County Council

Utting, W (1991) *Children in the Public Care.* HMSO

Warner, N (1992) *Choosing with Care.* HMSO

Preparing to Care

Please complete your personal details

Name . . . .

Post . . . .

Date of appointment . . . .

Line manager . . . .

Supervisor/s (if different from line manager) . . . .

. . . .

Module 1

Introduction to Module 1

Aim

To provide an introduction to the purpose and function of your home, including operational and personnel practices and procedures.

Module content

1.1   Staff, children, young people, organisation structure, and the home's statement of purpose and function

1.2   An introduction to the legal framework

1.3   Supervision

1.4   Health and safety

1.5   Personnel and welfare issues

1.6   Discipline and grievance procedures

1.7   Administration

        References

Completion

In order to complete module 1 effectively you will need to have access to:

- a staffing structure chart/diagram which applies to your organisation;

- your home's statement of purpose and function;   *National Minimum Standards*

- the Children Act 1989; *2004* + *Children's home regulations 2002*

- Department of Health Guidance and Regulations (see references);

- Appendix 1 - Residential Child Care: an introduction to the legal framework;

11

- your home's procedures manual;

- personnel documentation including grievance and disciplinary procedures and staff support.

If you are unable to find this material ask your supervisor where you might obtain it.

Module 1.1 Staff, children/young people, organisation structure, and the home's statement of purpose and function

Objectives

When you have completed this section you will be able to:

- *name all the staff in your home and state their job title;*

- *name all the children/young people in your residential home;*

- *demonstrate your understanding of lines of accountability, decision making and support using the organisation chart;*

- *demonstrate your understanding of the purpose and function of your home.*

Staff

Starting work in a residential home can be daunting. Remembering names is not always easy. One way to aid your memory is to write down the names of your colleagues and their positions and the names of children and young people.

Write in the space below the names of all the people who work in your home and their role and position. For example,

      Delroy Wilson -   manager
      Pauline Close   -   senior residential social worker
      Greg Greens   -   cook

(Further space is provided overleaf.)

Staff

(cont.)

Children and young people

Now complete a similar list for all the children/young people. For reasons of confidentiality you should use first names only for the children/young people. For example,

Stacy, Kelly, Paul, Femi, Manjeet, Kevin, Darren

Accountability

Before you started at the home, you should have received a staffing structure/organisation chart.

In the space below, use the chart to indicate the lines of accountability running through the staffing structure. Insert the names of post holders against the positions if they are not already there. You may want to attach your chart to this page as an *aide-mémoire*.

Statement of purpose and function

You should also have a copy of your home's statement of purpose and function. Each home is required by the Children Act 1989 and the associated guidance and regulations to state *what* kinds of services it provides for children and *why* and *how* such services are provided.

Record clearly in the space below your understanding of the purpose and function of your home and the service/s it provides for children/young people.

Evaluation 1.1

The following evaluation form is to be completed by your supervisor and is part of the process of monitoring your progress (see page 5, 'Supervision and evaluation', for an explanation of the learning criteria and method of use). Similar forms appear at the end of each section throughout the manual. The one below has been completed as an example.

Objectives	Acquaintance	Familiarity	Ability to use	Relative proficiency	Competence	Date	Date	Date
Staff and roles					✓	20.8.98		.
Residents' names					✓	20.8.98		
Lines of accountability				✓		20.8.98		
Purpose and function			✓			20.8.98		

Comments and signatures

The box below is for recording comments relevant to the evaluation of this section (similar boxes appear at the end of each section throughout the manual). Any comments should be signed both by you and by your supervisor.

Paul knows all the staff names and the names of children, and he understands the lines of accountability (though he hasn't yet met the external manager).

He understands the purpose and function of the home but does not yet feel confident to discuss these with anyone outside of the home. We will re-assess the purpose and function on 21.9.98.

Dave Brown   Paul Pinner

Evaluation 1.1

Objectives	Acquaintance	Familiarity	Ability to use	Relative proficiency	Competence	Date	Date	Date
Staff and roles								
Residents' names								
Lines of accountability								
Purpose and function								

Comments and signatures

Module 1.2 An introduction to the legal framework

Objectives

When you have completed this section you will be able to:

- *identify the legislation which determines the placement of children and young people in your home and their legal status;*

- *demonstrate your knowledge and understanding of the legislation, regulations and guidance which affect the running of residential homes.*

Children and young people who live in residential homes vary in age from birth to 18 years and over. The very youngest may be in a residential home such as a mother and baby home. The oldest, those above 16, may be in children's homes prior to returning home or moving towards independent living in the community. Children of all ages may live in residential settings such as local authority, voluntary and private children's homes, boarding schools, residential special schools and therapeutic community homes.

It is clear from the above, and from the introduction to the manual, that there is a wide range of residential provision for children and young people which aims to meet an equally wide range of needs.

Although each child/young person will have their own specific needs, there are needs which are common to all children being cared for in residential homes. Barbara Kahan in *Growing Up in Groups* (1994: 16) has summarised these needs.

> Whatever their ages or the settings in which they are being looked after, children and young people have common needs. The most important of these are for physical comfort, shelter, warmth and food; a stable environment to live in and to feel safe and secure; protection from abuse and ill-use; proper health care; education and the opportunity to fulfil their potential; personal privacy and space; association with and opportunity to make friends with children and young people of their own age; to feel valued by other people, particularly those who are significant to them, like parents or substitute parents. They also need clear boundaries, consistency in the care they receive and effective benevolent control.

In addition to these *general needs* children and young people will also have *specific needs* relating to their age, gender, 'race', religion, language, culture, physical, mental and emotional development and individual backgrounds.

19

There is legislation that determines where children and young people may be cared for when they live away from home. It is important to understand why and under which sections of the legislation the children and young people are placed in your home because this will in part determine their legal rights and the way you are able to work with them.

The following exercises will help you to identify the legal status of the children and young people cared for in residential homes. You may find the information in Appendix 1 - Residential Child Care: an introduction to the legal framework - and in Figure 1.2.1 below helpful when you complete the exercises.

Fig.1.2.1 Pathways to residential child care

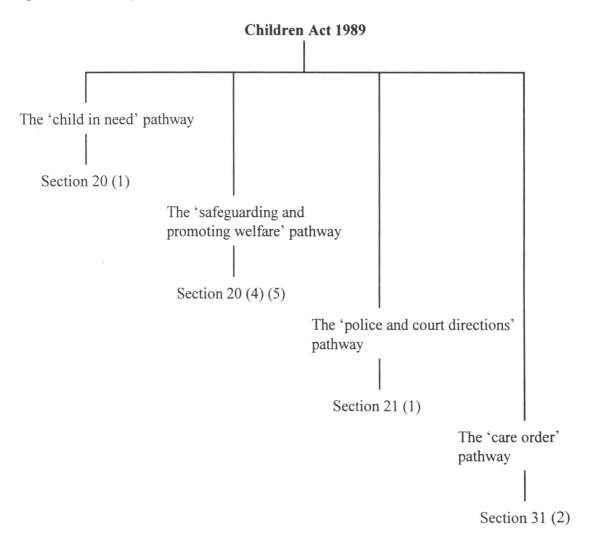

Children Act 1989

The 'child in need' pathway

Section 20 (1)

The 'safeguarding and promoting welfare' pathway

Section 20 (4) (5)

The 'police and court directions' pathway

Section 21 (1)

The 'care order' pathway

Section 31 (2)

Legal routes into residential care

Below are examples of the types of circumstances which may apply to some of the children and young people in residential homes. It may be the case that not all these examples apply in your home but you should complete them to demonstrate that you understand the legislation and the legal status of children living in residential homes. Record in the spaces provided the pathways 'Children in need', 'Safeguarding and promoting welfare', 'Police and court direction' or 'Care order and the Section(s) of the Children Act 1989 that applies.

Case A

Jane and Paul's mother has a medical condition which requires hospitalisation for some months. There are no other relatives who are able to care for Jane and Paul. Their mother has asked the social services department to care for them until she is fit again.

Legal pathway: . . . .

Relevant Section of the Children Act 1989: . . . .

Case B

Greg had a series of foster placements following the death of his parents. The placements were not successful due to Greg's volatile behaviour, his difficulty in settling in and his constant absconding. Greg has no relatives who can look after him and the courts have granted parental responsibility to the local authority who plan to provide a residential placement for Greg.

Legal pathway: . . . .

Relevant Section of the Children Act 1989: . . . .

Case C

Kate has been removed from her home by her social worker and the police as an emergency measure due to serious concerns that she is being physically abused and is at risk of serious harm.

Legal status: . . . .

Relevant Section of the Children Act 1989:

Case D

Peter has cerebral palsy and cannot be cared for by his mother who has two other children and is unable to provide the care that Peter needs. Peter's mother has asked the social services department to help in looking after him.

Legal status: . . . .

Relevant Section of the Children Act 1989: . . . .

Case E

Lorraine has been charged with several burglary offences. It is not possible for her to continue living at home for a variety of reasons. The court has adjourned the case for reports and has remanded her to local authority accommodation until her case can be heard for sentence.

Legal status: . . . .

Relevant Section of the Children Act 1989: . . . .

Residential homes are complex places in which to live and work as they serve two main functions. On the one hand they are homes for the children and young people and must therefore provide an environment which reflects the needs of the residents. The home should be attractive and free from health hazards. It should provide facilities for privacy and for entertaining visitors as well as space for quiet pursuits such as homework, reading and other activities. On the other hand they are places of employment for the staff who care for the children and young people and as such they must comply with a range of employment legislation.

An understanding of the legal framework within which residential homes operate is important because it will enable you to respond effectively and efficiently to the needs of the children and young people.

In thinking about the legal framework it may be useful to consider it as a pyramid of legislation. On top are the Acts: primary legislation passed by Parliament. Below them are regulations and schedules: secondary or subordinate legislation which supports the main Acts; then guidance. The Acts, regulations and schedules provide details of what *must* and what *can* be done. Guidance is the official advice on *how* to develop good practice. See Figure 1.2.2 for examples.

Your home will be inspected periodically by social services, health and safety, and fire inspectors. During the inspection processes attention will be paid to how closely current practice in your residential home relates to legislation and guidance in safeguarding and promoting the welfare and development of the children and young people.

Appendix 1 gives an overview of the legal framework. The most relevant regulations, schedules and guidance are contained in volumes 1 and 4 of *The Children Act 1989 Guidance and Regulations* (Department of Health, 1991a, 1991b). A copy of each of these will be available in your home. Your policy and procedures manual will also contain information on health and safety and fire regulations, and the statement of purpose and function will provide additional important information.

Fig.1.2.2. **Pyramid of legislation**

Acts
Primary legislation

e.g The Children Act 1989

Regulations and schedules
Subordinate legislation

e.g   Children's Homes Regulations 1991

Guidance
Developing best practice

e.g The Children Act 1989: Guidance and Regulations Volume 4 Residential Care

This relatively short section provides an introduction to help you to clarify the legal framework within which residential care operates. It is important to relate the legislation and guidance you examine here (and elsewhere in the manual) to your own practice and to the practice you observe in your home. This legal section also provides a backdrop against which all other sections in your manual may be viewed as you work your way through it - towards best practice.

Evaluation 1.2

Objectives	Acquaintance	Familiarity	Ability to use	Relative proficiency	Competence	Date	Date	Date
Identify legislation								
Demonstrate knowledge and understanding								

Comments and signatures

NB: Ensure all comments are signed by both you and your supervisor.

Module 1.3 Supervision

Objectives

When you have completed this section you will have:

- *stated the model/s of supervision used in your home;*

- *arranged a series of supervision dates.*

The Support Force for Children's Residential Care, in their publication *Staff Supervision in Children's Homes* (1995), identified three 'strands' that make up effective supervision in residential work with children and young people. These are:

- getting the work done;
- supporting staff;
- helping staff to develop and extend their individual skills and knowledge.

Throughout your induction you should be given information and feedback on your practice and your ability to deliver an effective and responsive service to the children and young people in your home. This may be done in a variety of ways. Your supervisor will use one 'model' of supervision, or a combination of 'models' which often includes:

- formal one-to-one supervision;
- informal on-the-spot guidance and/or discussion;
- group discussion.

Whichever model or combination of models your supervisor uses, he or she will be trying to address the three strands that will enable you to work effectively with the children and young people.

Your supervisor will also discuss the standard of your work, your personal development, your attendance and punctuality and the way you relate to your colleagues and the children and young people.

Effective supervision

Getting the work done

An effective residential social worker will carry out a number of tasks which are vital to the well- being and personal development of the children and young people in the residential home. Some are obvious, such as helping the children and young people prepare a meal; others are less tangible, such as helping a young person develop self-esteem and a clear sense of their own identity.

Support

In order to carry out the many and varied tasks effectively there should be a forum where you can discuss your work, including the things that concern you, and your emotional responses to the tasks, the children and young people and your colleagues.

Development

Supervision is also concerned with helping you to gain knowledge and develop skills which will enable you to be a more effective child care professional. For this reason you need to be an active participant in the supervision process. You must be prepared to raise the issues which you feel affect your practice, and be ready to contribute to resolving any problems. Your supervisor and colleagues will not know everything about you. Use your supervision opportunities to discuss your *strengths* as well as ways to *improve* your practice.

As you near the end of this module a formal supervision session will take place. If you have not already done so, use this opportunity to discuss with your manager the model or models of supervision used in your home, and record your understanding of them in the space provided on the following page.

Record below the supervision model/s used in your home.

Formal supervision sessions

Supervision sessions are built into your induction programme. The number of sessions you have as part of your induction will depend on the supervision model/s used in your home. Supervision will not cease at the end of your induction; it will be a part of your employment and will help you to develop and maintain a high standard of performance. Formal supervison is integral to your authority's/agency's appraisal policies.

You should use the space below to record the dates of your formal supervision sessions; these should be signed both by you and your supervisor.

Date	Supervisor	Signature	Signature

Evaluation 1.3

Objectives	Acquaintance	Familiarity	Ability to use	Relative proficiency	Competence	Date	Date	Date
Models of supervision								
Supervision dates								

Comments and signatures

Module 1.4 Health and safety

Objectives

When you have completed this section, you will be able to:

- *describe the emergency systems, including first aid, and demonstrate the use of emergency equipment;*

- *explain the policy on smoking;*

- *explain the policy on alcohol;*

- *describe the action you need to take in the event of an accident or assault at work.*

The residential home in which you work, while being home to the children and young people, is also a place of work for the staff and as such must comply with a range of health and safety regulations. The regulations help to create a safe environment.

The following exercises will help you to identify the range of safety equipment, systems and procedures used in your residential home.

Emergency equipment and procedures

In the event of an emergency prompt action often helps to minimise harm to individuals and/or damage to property. There is a range of emergency equipment kept and used in each residential home, for example keys, fire extinguishers, fire blankets. It is important that you know how to use the equipment before you meet a real emergency.

Record overleaf the different procedures in use in your home and ask your supervisor to sign and date when you have completed your demonstration of the relevant equipment.

Emergency procedures

What procedures could you use in the following situations?

- a sudden illness requiring first aid

- a serious accident requiring a hospital visit

- **disruptive behaviour which threatens to, or leads to, serious disorder**

- **suspicion of intruder/s on the premises**

Fire detection and fire fighting equipment

It is important that all staff are familiar with the fire detection and fire fighting equipment as well as evacuation procedures and routes. In the event of a fire, prompt action will save lives and prevent serious damage.

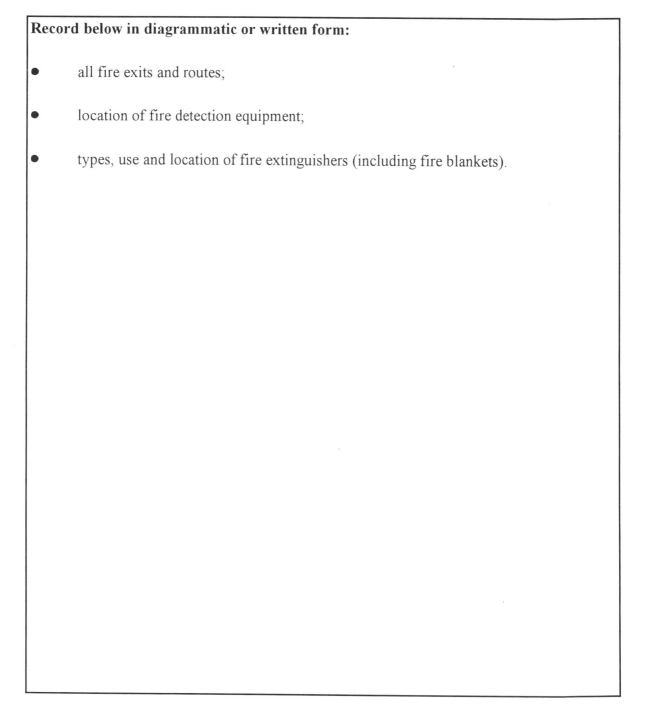

Record below in diagrammatic or written form:

- all fire exits and routes;

- location of fire detection equipment;

- types, use and location of fire extinguishers (including fire blankets).

Fire detection and fighting equipment, exit routes and evacuation procedures (cont.)

What signals will you receive if there is a fire?

What should you do if you receive the signal?

You will be asked to demonstrate the use of emergency and security equipment. When you have completed your demonstration your supervisor should sign and date your file (below) to indicate your competence. All the following equipment may not be present in your residential home and you may have equipment which is not included here. The important thing, however, is that you are familiar with all of the equipment available in your residential home which you may be required to use.

Emergency equipment

	Date	Supervisor's signature
1. Room call system, such as:		
Buzzers	. . . .	
Others	. . . .	
	. . . .	
2. Emergency call system, such as:		
Personal alarms	. . . .	
Emergency call buttons	. . . .	
Others	. . . .	
	. . . .	
3. Systems for fire detection and evacuation:		
Smoke detectors	. . . .	
Fire alarm switches	. . . .	
Control panels	. . . .	
Fire extinguishers	. . . .	

	Date	Supervisor's signature
Fire blankets	. . . .	
Evacuation procedures	. . . .	

First aid

The Health and Safety Act (1974) recommends that there should always be one person on duty with a recognised first aid qualification and that everyone should be aware of who that person is. This enables other staff to contact them in an emergency.

Who are the first aiders?

Who are the 'appointed persons' in your residential home?

Where are the first aid kits kept?

Who is responsible for maintaining the kits?

Smoking policy

The health risks from smoking tobacco are well documented and there is increasing evidence to support the risks associated with passive smoking. Local authorities have a clear responsibility to promote the health of the children and young people in their care and should ensure that the staff in residential homes actively promote the benefits of not smoking (please refer to Department of Health, 1994). Your home should have a smoking policy that aims to protect children, young people and staff from the effects of tobacco smoke. The smoking policy should include the arrangements (if any) made for the children and young people, staff and visitors to smoke while in the home and the steps which are taken to promote the benefits of not smoking.

Complete the following statements:

Staff can/cannot*smoke in the residential home.

If staff can smoke they may smoke in . . . .

They may have . . . . smoking breaks during the shift.

They can/cannot* smoke in front of the children and young people.

Staff can/cannot* offer a cigarette to children and young people.

If children and young people can smoke they may smoke in . . . .

Children and young people must be . . . years old to smoke cigarettes in the residential home. The exceptions to this are:

. . . .

. . . .

. . . .

Staff can/cannot* buy cigarettes for children and young people.

Staff can/cannot* give gifts of cigarettes to children and young people.

If visitors wish to smoke they may smoke in . . . .

(Continued on next page.)

41

The benefits of not smoking are promoted in the following ways:

. . . .

. . . .

. . . .

. . . .

. . . .

. . . .

. . . .

* delete where appropriate

Alcohol policy

There are health risks associated with drinking alcohol. Consuming alcohol, even in small quantities, reduces concentration and impairs responses. Sustained drinking can lead to alcohol dependence and other health risks, and intoxication can lead to behaviours that put the individual or others at risk of harm. Each home will have an alcohol policy that aims to protect children, young people and staff from the effects of drinking alcohol.

By completing the following statements you should be able to clarify your home's policy on alcohol. They are based on the Dept of Health Guidelines on Smoking and Alcohol Consumption in Residential Child Care Establishments (1994).

Complete the following statements:

Staff can/cannot* drink alcohol in the residential home.

If staff can drink alcohol they may do so in the following circumstances:

Children/young people can/cannot* drink alcohol in the residential home.

* delete as appropriate

(Continued on next page.)

If children/young people can drink alcohol in the home they may do so in the following circumstances:

NB: If drinking alcohol is permitted the policy should make it clear that:

staff should ensure that they and the children and young people do not consume alcohol to the extent that they experience intoxication or any impaired response;

no more than one-third of members of staff on duty should consume alcohol. At least two staff members on duty must abstain;

alcohol should not be stored in the residential home.

Accident or assault at work

In the event of an accident it is important to follow the correct procedures for a number of reasons.

●   It is good child care and staff practice.

●   It is a legal requirement of the Health and Safety Executive.

●   If serious/permanent injury results, you or the children and young people may need to be compensated. You may also need some time off work to recuperate.

●   To help prevent the same thing happening again.

Unless the correct procedures are followed you may jeopardise your entitlement to sick leave or compensation, and/or be held responsible for negligence.

In the following exercise a number of scenarios are proposed. Record what you would do in each of the situations, using the space provided.

●   **You trip over loose carpet and fall over but you detect no injury:**

●   **The day after you fell over the carpet you discover a painful swelling on your elbow:**

(Continued on the next page.)

- **While helping a child/young person with her craftwork the Stanley knife she is using slips and cuts her thumb:**

- **A child/young person slips on the wet floor in the bathroom/shower and grazes her shin:**

- **During a fight between two young people you help your colleagues pull them apart. One of the young people lashes out and a blow catches you on the side of your head. You help to see the incident through but then realise you have a really bad headache:**

(Continued on next page.)

- **Two weeks after the fight incident you have severe headaches; the doctor has suggested that you have some time off work:**

- **You have to refuse a young person's request who, disappointed and angry by your response, punches you on the arm:**

Evaluation 1.4

Objectives	Acquaintance	Familiarity	Ability to use	Relative proficiency	Competence	Date	Date	Date
Emergency procedures								
Emergency equipment								
Smoking policy								
Alcohol policy								
Accident/ assault at work								

Comments and signatures

Module 1.5 Personnel and welfare issues

Objectives

When you have completed this section you will be able to explain personnel policies, practices and procedures in relation to:

- *pay, expenses and pensions;*

- *annual leave;*

- *welfare services;*

- *support/counselling meetings;*

- *sickness procedures;*

- *internal/external communication;*

- *use of your own car;*

- *loss/damage to personal effects.*

Your authority/agency will have policies which cover personnel and welfare issues, and procedures for ensuring that such policies are applied effectively. These can usually be obtained from the staffing or personnel department. However, ploughing your way through masses of policies and procedures may not be the most useful way of acquainting yourself with the nuts and bolts of how they actually work.

The examples used in the exercises on the following pages have actually occurred in some residential homes. State the course of action you would take in each situation.

Pay, expenses and pensions

You have been allocated the wrong tax code what should you do?

You worked an extra shift last Wednesday which was agreed with your line manager as overtime. Fill in the overtime claim form, using your current overtime rate. Ask your supervisor to check your completed form and sign and date below.

Signed   Date

Overtime claim form completed: . . . .

What will you do with the claim form now?

You want to join your authority's pension scheme. What should you do?

You are due a salary increment which has not been added to your pay. What should you do?

Leave entitlement

Your annual leave entitlement is . . . . . . days.

This is inclusive/exclusive* of bank holidays.

You want to take one week's leave at Easter, two weeks in the summer and one at Christmas. You are prepared to be flexible with any remaining leave. Describe below the procedure for booking your leave.

Your manager cannot/will not agree to the two weeks you want in the summer. What can you do?

* delete the one that does not apply

Welfare services

Many authorities recognise that from time to time we all encounter situations in our lives which throw us off balance and they try to help by providing a service to their employees. The welfare service is a confidential one and may be able to help you with a range of difficulties, including financial and other domestic matters.

How can you contact your welfare service?

What criteria are used to determine how often you can see the welfare officer?

Support/counselling

The work you will be doing can bring many rewards in helping children and young people to develop and reach their potential. It can also stretch your emotional resources. Your employing authority or agency may provide a support system to help you should you need it.

What support does your authority provide? How can you gain access to it?

Sickness procedures

If you already work for the authority you may be familiar with the procedures for reporting sickness. If not, you need to become familiar with them. The following exercise is useful in either case.

Imagine the following scenario:

It's Thursday night and all day you've felt unwell. Fortunately you were on an early shift and left work before your symptoms deteriorated. By 9.30 p.m. you think it unlikely that you'll be well enough to go in for your shift tomorrow. On waking the following morning, your fears are confirmed you are too ill to go to work.

Describe, either using a flow chart or in writing, what procedure you will follow, from the point you decide that you are unable to attend work to your first day back at work.

Internal/external communication

Notice boards

> You have been given a few flyers for an excellent training course which you believe your colleagues and others in the residential home may find interesting/useful. Where can you display them?
>
>
>
> Where can the children and young people display their school work or things that interest them?
>
>
>
>
>
> What other kinds of information would it be useful to display?

Using your own vehicle for authority business

Occasionally it may be necessary for you to use your own vehicle to carry out the business of the home. Record below the policy and procedures that relate to the use of personal vehicles.

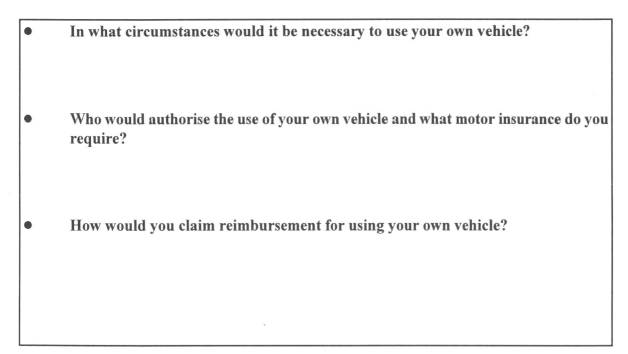

- **In what circumstances would it be necessary to use your own vehicle?**

- **Who would authorise the use of your own vehicle and what motor insurance do you require?**

- **How would you claim reimbursement for using your own vehicle?**

Loss/damage to personal effects

Your managers expect you to take every precaution to safeguard your personal possessions. While at work your personal belongings may be lost or damaged. There are a number of precautions to be taken when working in a residential home which will minimise the risk of loss or damage to your personal effects.

- Do not wear expensive clothes/jewellery while on shift.
- Do not bring valuables into the home.

In the event of loss or damage while on duty, you may be entitled to a replacement or the cost of repairing the damage. Record your home's policy by answering the questions below in the space provided.

- **What can you be reimbursed for?**

- **How do you make a claim?**

Evaluation 1.5

Objectives	Acquaintance	Familiarity	Ability to use	Relative proficiency	Competence	Date	Date	Date
Pay, expenses and pensions								
Annual leave								
Welfare services								
Support/ counselling meetings								
Sickness procedures								
Internal/ external communication								
Use of your own car								
Loss/damage to personal effects								

Comments and signatures

Module 1.6 Discipline and grievance procedures

Objectives

When you have completed this section you will be able to explain what will happen if:

● *disciplinary action is necessary;*

● *you have a complaint about an issue concerning your workplace.*

'Discipline' is defined by the Oxford Dictionary as 'attempt to improve the behaviour of one self or another by training or rules'. The disciplinary procedures are designed to help staff perform to an acceptable level in all areas of their work. It is not meant as a stick with which to beat you; it is a tool to help you fulfil your potential.

'Grievance' is defined as having 'cause for complaint'. If you have any complaints there is a set of procedures for addressing them. It is advisable that you become familiar with them to enable any complaints you may have to be dealt with as quickly as possible.

Disciplinary procedures

There are a number of behaviours for which disciplinary or corrective action may need to be taken.

Below is a list of such situations:

● You are consistently late.

● Your performance does not meet the required standard.

● You arrive at work inappropriately dressed.

● Your sickness days exceed the acceptable limits.

On the following pages, space is provided for you to describe in writing or using a flow chart what action may be taken in each case. The response to the first situation - you are consistently late - is provided as an example.

You are consistently late:

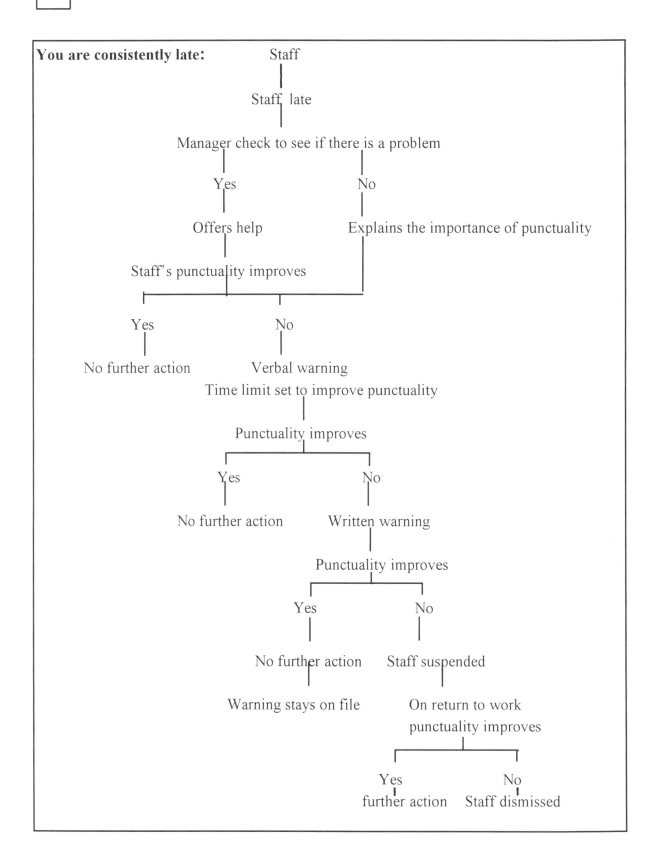

Your performance does not meet the required standard:

You arrive at work inappropriately dressed:

Your sickness days exceed the acceptable limits:

Gross misconduct

There are some behaviours which are referred to as 'gross misconduct'. They will usually all be dealt with in a similar way.

List below all behaviours your authority/agency defines as gross misconduct:

Are the procedures for dealing with them all the same? If they are not all dealt with in the same way, group together the ones which are and outline the procedures for each group of behaviours in the space provided on the next page.

Procedures for gross misconduct:

Grievance procedures

If you have a complaint about an issue in your workplace you will find that your authority or agency has a procedure for addressing it.

The following exercise will help you to identify some of the things you may complain about.

Put a 'T' in the relevant box if the statement is true and an 'F' if it is false:

I can make a complaint about:

safety issues in the home ☐

lack of parking facilities ☐

lack of nursery provisions for my children ☐

the quality of meals ☐

the language my colleagues use ☐

equal opportunities issues in the authority ☐

(for example sexual or racial harassment from colleagues or from children and young people)

In the space provided on the next page, record the way you would go about making two types of complaint - one about a colleague, another about your manager.

If you have a complaint about a colleague, what can you do?

If you have a complaint about your manager, what can you do?

It is possible to make a complaint about almost anything in the workplace. However, often a quiet word in the ear of the person concerned will achieve the desired result.

Evaluation 1.6

Objectives	Acquaintance	Familiarity	Ability to use	Relative proficiency	Competence	Date	Date	Date
Explain disciplinary procedures								
Explain grievance procedures								

Comments and signatures

Module 1.7 Administration

Objectives

When you have completed this section you will be able to:

● *state the procedure for ordering stationery;**

● *explain how to access the photocopier and demonstrate how to use your home/centre's photocopier and fax;**

● *carry out petty cash transactions;*

● *explain the system for helping children/young people keep their money safe.*

An efficient home needs good administrative support. If you have administrative support workers they will be helped by residential social workers supplying them with correct information in a format they find useful. For this reason you need to be familiar with your home's administrative procedures. These include:

● ordering and using stationery;
● photocopying and faxing;
● the petty cash system;
● children and young people's money.

Ordering and using stationery

Where are the general items of stationery kept?
How do you gain access to them?

* may not apply to smaller homes

Photocopying and sending and receiving fax messages

Do you have unlimited access to photocopying facilities?   yes ☐   no ☐

Do you have unlimited access to the facsimile?   yes ☐   no ☐

If no, how do you gain access to the photocopier, *or* get material photocopied *or* send/receive a fax?

Note: You will need to take account of the policy and practice regarding confidentiality.

Procedure for using photocopier and fax:

With guidance from your supervisor or the administrative staff, photocopy a sample of the documents you would normally be required to copy, and send a fax.

Your supervisor will sign and date when this has been successfully achieved.

Signed: . . . . **Date:** . . . .

Petty cash

It is often necessary to hold a small amount of money in the home for immediate use. This is called petty cash.

What are the main uses of petty cash in your home?

- ....

- ....

- ....

- ....

- ....

- ....

- ....

What is your home's policy on personal loans from petty cash?

Who has access to petty cash?

NB: It is important that the staff's personal money is kept separate from that of the residential home.

In consultation with your supervisor carry out two petty cash transactions. Record these on the form below. Your supervisor will sign and date them when they have been successfully completed.

Type of transaction	Signed	Date

Note: Your supervisor may wish to see more than two transactions.

Children and young people's money

The children and young people in your home will often have money of their own such as pocket money, gifts from relatives or money that they have earned or saved. Your home will have a system for helping the children and young people to keep their money safe. Explain this system by answering the questions in the box below.

How do the children and young people receive their pocket money?

Where is it kept?

How do they gain access to it?

How are the children and young people encouraged to keep their money safe?

Evaluation 1.7

Objectives	Acquaintance	Familiarity	Ability to use	Relative proficiency	Competence	Date	Date	Date
Ordering Stationery								
Using fax and photocopier								
Petty cash transactions								
Children and young people's money								

Comments and signatures

References

Children Act 1989. HMSO

Department of Health (1991a) *The Children Act 1989 Guidance and Regulations: Volume 1 Court Orders.* HMSO

Department of Health (1991b) *The Children Act 1989 Guidance and Regulations: Volume 4 Residential Care.* HMSO

Department of Health (1994) *Guidelines on Smoking and Alcohol Consumption in Residential Child-Care Establishments.* HMSO

Health and Safety at Work Act 1974. HMSO

Kahan, B (1994) *Growing Up in Groups.* HMSO

Support Force for Children's Residential Care (1995) *Staff Supervision in Children's Homes.* SFCRC

Module 2

Introduction to Module 2

Aim

To develop the knowledge and core skills necessary to safeguard and promote the welfare of children and young people in residential homes.

Module content

2.1   Safeguarding and promoting the welfare of children and young people

2.2   Dignity, privacy, confidentiality and safety

2.3   Ethnicity, religion, culture and language

2.4   Admissions and discharges

2.5   Disciplinary and control measures

2.6   Working in partnership with families

2.7   Going out and coming home

2.8   Recording and report writing

2.9   Care planning and reviews

2.10   Health

2.11   Education

2.12   Comments, compliments and complaints

2.13   Meetings

2.14   Moving on

       References

Completion

In order to complete module 2 effectively you will need to have access to:

- the appendices at the end of this manual;

- Department of Health (1991a) *The Children Act 1989 Guidance and Regulations Volume 1: Court Orders;*

- Department of Health (1991b) *The Children Act 1989 Guidance and Regulations Volume 4: Residential Care;*

- your home's policy and procedures manual;

- the Children Act 1989;

- Department of Health (1993) *Guidance on Permissible Forms of Control in Children's Residential Care;*

- Department of Health (1995a) *Looking After Children: Assessment and Action Records;*

- Department of Health (1997) *The Control of Children in the Public Care: Interpretation of the Children Act 1989.*

You may also find it useful to consult the following publications and the texts referred to throughout module 2:

- Kahan, B (1994) *Growing Up in Groups;*

- Area Child Protection Committee Policy and Procedures

- Department of Health (1994) *Standards for Residential Child Care Services;*

- Children's Home Regulations 1991;

- Review of Children's Cases Regulations 1991;

- The United Nations Convention on the Rights of the Child 1989;

- Department of Health (1995c) *The Health of the Young Nation;*

- Access to Personal Files (Social Services) Regulations 1989;

- Access to Personal Files Act 1987.

Module 2.1 Safeguarding and promoting the welfare of children and young people

Objectives

When you have completed this section you will be able to:

- *identify the methods, structures, practices and procedures for safeguarding and promoting the welfare of the children and young people in your residential home;*

- *explain what action you would take in a range of situations in order to safeguard and promote children/young people's welfare;*

- *explain the circumstances in which physical restraint may be used.*

Safeguarding and promoting the welfare of children and young people is a legal requirement of the Children Act 1989 and is central to the duties of all staff who are working with children. It is the foundation upon which all interaction and intervention with the children and young people must be based.

This section concentrates on structures which support staff in their duty to safeguard and promote the welfare of children and young people, and the practice and procedures which must be implemented when there is cause for concern. In addition to the Department of Health *Regulations and Guidance*, this section is informed by Barbara Kahan's book *Growing Up in Groups* (1994).

Think about the structures, systems and routines in your home and consider how supportive they are in safeguarding and promoting the welfare of children and young people. Do they create an atmosphere that is pleasant and safe, and which allows for the physical and emotional growth and development of the children and young people? Do they respect the dignity of children and young people, provide for their rights and help them to participate fully in their care?

Supportive structure

A supportive structure is one where staff are encouraged to be open about their day-to-day practice within the staff group, where they can share problems and think about solutions, and where they can receive constructive feedback on their performance. This process does not end with the probationary period and applies to everyone in the team. Effective supervision and regular staff meetings enable the staff team to develop and maintain coherent and consistent responses to the care of the children and young people.

Does your home have a supportive structure? Are you able to share problems and solutions in a range of settings? Record the types of support setting available in your home by ticking the appropriate box or boxes below.

84

Practice and principles for safeguarding and promoting the welfare of children and young people

Are there methods of working and principles operating in your home that are agreed by all staff (and where possible children and young people) which are consistent with safeguarding and promoting the welfare of children and young people? Examples are listed in the box below and space is provided for you to add others that you have noted in your home. Safeguarding and promoting the welfare of children and young people underpins all the sections in this manual.

- **Appropriate gender mix of shift team.**

- **Minimum use of sanctions and physical controls by avoiding unnecessary confrontation and provocation.**

- **Supervision of children and young people:**
  inside the home;
  outside of the home where appropriate.

- **A forum is provided for constructive feedback on the interactions of staff with children and young people.**

- **Children and young people have access to ChildLine and other relevant helplines, independent visitors, advocates, children's rights officer, specialist counsellors.**

- **Guidance is offered on appropriate touching.**

- **Training is provided in child protection issues and procedures.**

- **Training is provided in appropriate physical control methods.**

- **Written procedural guidance acknowledges the possibility that children and young people may be abused in the home.**

- **Staff monitor visitors to the home.**

(Continued on next page.)

- **Constructive resolution of conflict between children and young people and staff.**

- **Effective methods of addressing bullying.**

- **Effective methods of addressing sexism and racism.**

- **Effective methods of addressing harassment.**

- **Others (list here further practices/principles in operation in your home).**

Child Protection

It is essential that *all* staff working with children and young people in residential care are aware of the possibility of abuse of the children and young people and are familiar with the relevant child protection procedures.

It is likely that some children and young people in the residential home have experienced or are experiencing abuse. Residential care should provide an environment in which children and young people feel safe enough to disclose previous or current abuse.

In seeking to safeguard and promote the welfare of the children and young people you need to be aware of the possibility of abuse outside of and within the residential home, by family, friends, other residents, visitors and staff.

You should be given very clear guidance on what to do if a child or young person discloses to you their experience of abuse, past or current. You should also be given guidance on what to do if you suspect that any child or young person is experiencing abuse.

You need to be alert to:

- the *current* behaviour of the children, young people and staff in the residential home;

- the *current* nature of contacts outside of the home - for instance with family members, friends and associates of the children/young people;

- records of events *prior to the child/young person's admission* which may put them at risk.

When working with children and young people it may sometimes be difficult to draw a line between behaviours regarded as 'normal' for the client group and behaviours which have 'gone too far'. Written guidance should be available which addresses the boundaries between 'normal' behaviour and behaviour which is abusive. Such issues should also be discussed in supervision sessions and staff meetings to ensure that all staff are clear about which behaviours are acceptable and which are not.

If you are concerned about any behaviour you have observed, or which a child or young person reports to you, you should discuss this with a senior member of staff or your manager as quickly as possible. If you are concerned about the behaviour of your manager you should discuss this with the external manager or any member of the Child Protection Team.

87

The following exercise describe a series of situations involving child protection issues. With reference to your home's child protection procedures describe the action you should take in each case. Your home's child protection procedures are based on your area child protection procedures. You may need to refer directly to these and any other relevant material. You should also refer to your authority's child protection procedures and any other relevant policy and/or procedure. (Please note that in cases when you are working with children and young people who have been placed from other areas, the child/young person's referring authority may investigate incidents using their own child protection procedures.)

You receive a call from someone saying she is the aunt of one of the children and would like to know if the child is at school today. She wants to pay her a surprise visit. She is not someone known to the staff.

Sharma, who is usually eager to take part in organised activities, has started spending a lot of time in her room away from the group. This seems to have coincided with the admission of Darren two weeks ago. She participates in activities if he is not involved.

Jamie, aged 10, on return from having spent the weekend at home talks excitedly about his uncle's fight with his dad. He thinks it's great because his dad won this time whereas he lost last time. Jamie can't wait until the next time to see who will win.

You notice that Brian has bruising on his back. He is not able to explain how he got it because he has speech difficulties.

You notice bruises on Maria's arm. On questioning her she discloses that Sarah, another resident, has been pinching her and has threatened to do much worse if she tells anyone. She begs you not to tell anyone.

While shopping with Debbie she tells you that she used to have sex with the proprietor of the newsagent's shop because he was kind and gave her cigarettes and sweets. Debbie is 14 years old and known to have told stories which have later proved to be untrue.

It is nearly bedtime in the home. Kenny has been argumentative and unsettled for the greater part of the evening, pacing around and trying to disturb other children and young people. Your colleague, Jim, who has been interacting with Kenny most of the evening, asks him to go to bed. As Kenny goes through the door he becomes verbally abusive to Jim, and turns and spits in his face. In what appears to be a brief moment of anger Jim slaps Kenny's face and, fearing retaliation, pulls the door shut. You are the only one to witness this. Jim has been severely provoked.

Procedures for refusing visits

Phong's father, who has been refused contact with his daughter by a court, has arrived for a visit. What responses can you make?

What might Phong learn from your responses?

Allegations made against staff

If a child/young person makes an allegation of abuse against a member of staff it could have a very distressing effect on the child who has made the allegation, and the person against whom the allegation is made, and a destructive impact on the home, unless there is careful planning for the enquiries. Your authority's/agency's procedures should make clear the need for two types of enquiries in the event of such an allegation:

- child protection enquiries, which may include police investigation of crime;

- staff disciplinary investigation.

These will often be taking place simultaneously and, while some disruption to the home will be inevitable, it is important to bear in mind that such allegations must be taken seriously and investigated sensitively as the child/young person's welfare is the principal concern.

However, everyone has a right to support the child or young person making the allegation and the person against whom the allegation is made. The welfare service or your authority's/agency's external support service may be a useful source of support for the member of staff. Union representatives or professional associations will also provide advice and representation for staff. The child or young person should receive support from individuals that they trust.

Every effort will be made to conduct the enquiries as quickly and as sensitively as possible to ensure the safety and well-being of all concerned.

Physically restraining children and young people (see also section 2.5)

The main duty of all staff is to safeguard the welfare of the children and young people in their care by providing a safe environment. This is the basis of good child care practice. You have a duty to ensure that the children and young people are protected from physically harming themselves or others. Your employing authority/agency has a duty to ensure that staff take reasonable and necessary action to prevent such harm, and to provide relevant training which will enable staff to do so.

There may be occasions when the only reasonable and necessary action is to physically restrict the movement of a child or young person. It may also be necessary on occasions to restrict the movement of a child or young person in order to prevent them causing serious damage to property in the home. The Department of Health has prepared written guidance (*Guidance on Permissible Forms of Control in Children's Residential Care*, 1993; *The Control of Children in the Public Care: Interpretation of the Children Act 1989*, 1997) and training material (*Taking Care, Taking Control*, 1996) which explain the circumstances that might justify physical restraint and the safe methods of restraint that may be used. You should ensure that you are familiar with

96

these, together with your home's policy on the physical restraint of children and young people.

Being involved in or witnessing such action, however necessary, can arouse strong emotions in everyone concerned. You should be given the opportunity to discuss the need for the use of restraint on each occasion it is used, and whether any other action could have been taken, and also have a forum within which to discuss your feelings and responses to such incidents. It is important that children and young people who have been restrained, or who have witnessed restraint, are provided with similar opportunities.

By discussing these issues with your supervisor and colleagues you will gain greater insight into the use of restraint as a caring act which helps to provide a safe environment for everyone in the home. If you observe anyone restraining a child/young person in a manner which gives you cause for concern you should discuss this with your colleagues, manager or external manager at the earliest opportunity.

In the exercises on the following two pages, record your understanding of restraint in terms of the questions posed.

When might it be neccessary to physically restrain a child or young person?

How can you safely restrain a child or young person?

(Continued on next page.)

What emotions may you experience as a result of observing, or being involved in, restraining a child or young person?

What emotions may the child or young person experience as a result of being restrained?

What emotions may children/young people experience as a result of witnessing restraint?

What action should be taken after a restraint incident to support (a) the child (b) the staff?

(Continued on next page.)

What might be done to avert the use of physical restraint?

If other children and young people are present during a physical restraint what, if anything, can be done to divert them away from the situation?

Evaluation 2.1

Objectives	Acquaintance	Familiarity	Ability to use	Relative proficiency	Competence	Date	Date	Date
Structures, methods and procedures for safeguarding and promoting welfare								
Suggested action								
Physical restraint								

Comments and signatures

Module 2.2 Dignity, privacy, confidentiality and safety

Objectives

When you have completed this section you will be able to:

- *identify your home procedures for ensuring dignity, privacy, confidentiality and safety of the children and young people;*

- *assess the effectiveness of these procedures;*

- *make suggestions for improvements.*

Residential care aims to provide an environment within which children and young people can develop and mature. As part of this process they will learn to show respect for, and sensitivity to, the needs of others and of themselves. To assist this learning process it is vital that they *experience* respect and sensitivity from everyone involved in providing for their care. Practical demonstration is often the most powerful method of creating a culture within which personal dignity and respect may develop.

The need to safeguard and promote the welfare of children and young people in residential care means that staff have to be especially vigilant that the children and young people's dignity, privacy, confidentiality and safety are not compromised.

Measures in place in your home

In this section, and the one which follows, you will need to assess critically the measures in place in your home for ensuring the children and young people's dignity, privacy, confidentiality and safety and to make suggestions, where appropriate, for improvements.

The following exercises cover a range of areas of concern regarding the dignity, privacy, confidentiality and safety offered to children and young people in residential homes. Consider current practice in your home regarding each area and record your observations in the space provided using the following criteria.

1.   Identify current practice (what policies and procedures are in place).

2.   Assess their effectiveness:

- Are the children and young people aware of the practice and procedures?
- Were they consulted in setting them up?
- Do they use the procedures?
- How are they assisted and supported?
- Are they satisfied with the procedures?
- Do the procedures safeguard and promote the welfare of the children/young people?

3.   Can any improvements be made to the procedures?

Often a new eye can see things in a different light. Your manager, colleagues and the children and young people will welcome suggestions for improving practice.

Personal time alone

1. **How does your home provide for the dignity, privacy, confidentiality and safety of the children and young people who want to spend time on their own away from the group?**

2. **Are these measures effective?**

3. **Have you any suggestions for improvements?**

Daily routines

1. **How does your home provide for dignity, privacy, confidentiality and safety of the children and young people in the following activities:**

   ● **waking up;**
   ● **bedtime;**
   ● **washing and bathing;**
   ● **personal hygiene?**

(Continued on the next page.)

2.   Are these measures effective?

3.   Have you any suggestions for improvement?

Visitors

1.   **How does your home provide for the dignity, privacy, confidentiality and safety of the children and young people when they have visitors?**

2.   **Are these measures effective?**

3.   **Have you any suggestions for improvement?**

Case notes

1. **How does your home respect dignity, privacy, confidentiality and safety in the way that children and young people's case notes are prepared and shared?**

2. **Are these measures effective?**

3. **Have you any suggestions for improvement?**

Medical needs

1.   **How does your home provide for the dignity, privacy, confidentiality and safety of the children and young people when making provision for their medical needs?**

2.   **Are these measures effective?**

3.   **Have you any suggestions for improvement?**

Telephone calls

1. How does your home provide for the dignity, privacy, confidentiality and safety of the children and young people when they make or receive phone calls?

2. Are these measures effective?

3. Have you any suggestions for improvement?

Mail

1.	**How does your home provide for the dignity, privacy, confidentiality and safety of the children and young people when they send and receive mail?**
2.	**Are these measures effective?**
3.	**Have you any suggestions for improvement?**

Searches

1.   **How does your home provide for the dignity, privacy, confidentiality and safety of the children and young people if it becomes necessary to search a child or young person's room?**

2.   **Are these measures effective?**

3.   **Have you any suggestions for improvement?**

Complaints

1. **How does your home provide for the dignity, privacy, confidentiality and safety of a child or young person who wishes to make a complaint?**

2. **Are these measures effective?**

3. **Have you any suggestions for improvement?**

Good practice checklist

Did you include some of the following in your answers? (Taken from Department of Health *Standards for Residential Child Care Services* (1994).)

- Staff respect children and young people's privacy through the way they address them and seek permission if they are encroaching on their privacy.

- Staff are provided with procedural guidance on privacy, confidentiality and access to records.

- Staff confirm they understand the guidance.

- Staff are sensitive to gender issues particularly when dealing with children and young people of the opposite sex.

- Staff are sensitive to issues of ethnicity, culture, religion, language (see 2.3).

- Staff knock on bedroom doors and wait for a reply before entering.

- Children and young people are encouraged to write letters in private.

- Children and young people are able to use a conveniently sited telephone in private.

- Children and young people are able to meet privately with their parents and others.

- Confidential papers are stored securely.

Evaluation 2.2

Objectives	Acquaintance	Familiarity	Ability to use	Relative proficiency	Competence	Date	Date	Date
Identify procedures for ensuring dignity, privacy confidentiality and safety of children and young people								
Assess effectiveness								
Suggestions for improvements								

Comments and signatures

Module 2.3 Ethnicity, religion, culture and language

Objectives

When you have completed this section you will be able to describe how your home provides for:

- *religious observance for the children and young people;*

- *cultural diversity;*

- *the specific dietary and physical care of children and young people from different backgrounds;*

- *practice which is not discriminatory.*

Outcomes for children and young people will be enhanced if 'the home makes positive arrangements to help children observe and preserve their religious, ethnic, cultural and linguistic identity and heritage' (Department of Health, *Standards for Residential Child Care Services* (1994)).

There are statutory requirements which address the ethnic, religious, cultural and linguistic backgrounds of children and young people living away from home. Examples of these can be found in the *Children's Homes Regulations 1991*, 11, 12(3), and in the Children Act 1989, sections 22(5)(c) and 64(3)(c).

Measures in place in your home

The statutory requirements regarding ethnic, religious, cultural and linguistic issues are a base from which to develop good practice. Each residential home should have its own procedures and practices for helping children and young people to develop a positive sense of identity.

As in the last section, a series of exercises follow but this time they specifically address issues of ethnicity, religion, culture and language as they are dealt with by procedures and practices in your home. Record your observations of current practice in your home and any suggestions you may have for improvement using the following criteria.

1.   **Identify current practice (what systems are in place).**

2.   **Assess their effectiveness**:

        Are the children and young people aware of the law, policies and procedures?
        Were they consulted about setting up the policies and procedures?
        Do they use the procedures?
        Are they satisfied with the procedures?

3.   **Can any improvements be made to the policies, practices and procedures?**
        Often a new eye sees things differently. Your manager, colleagues and the children and
        young people will welcome suggestions on how practice can be improved.

Religious observance

1.   **How does your home provide for religious observance?**

2.   **Are these measures effective?**

3.   **Have you any suggestions for improvement?**

Cultural diversity

Multicultural society

1. **How is a multicultural society reflected, supported and celebrated in your home?**

2. **Are these measures effective?**

3. **Have you any suggestions for improvement?**

Multicultural clothing

1. **How are children and young people helped to buy and wear clothes to reflect their culture?**

2. **Are these measures effective?**

3. **Have you any suggestions for improvement?**

Dietary requirements and physical care

Dietary requirements

1.	**How are the dietary needs and preferences of children/young people with different cultural backgrounds provided for?**
2.	**Are these measures effective?**
3.	**Have you any suggestions for improvement?**

Physical care

1. **How are the special hair and skin care needs of children and young people from African-Caribbean backgrounds met?**

2. **Are these measures effective?**

3. **Have you any suggestions for improvement?**

Non-discriminatory practice

1. **How do you and your colleagues ensure that children and young people receive equal quality of opportunity during their placement in your home?**

2. **Are these measures effective?**

3. **Have you any suggestions for improvement?**

Evaluation 2.3

Objectives	Acquaintance	Familiarity	Ability to use	Relative proficiency	Competence	Date	Date	Date
Religious observance for children and young people								
Cultural diversity								
Dietary and physical care								
Non-discriminatory practice								

Comments and signature

Module 2.4 Admissions and discharges

Objectives

When you have completed this section you will be able to:

- *state the criteria for admission to your residential home;*

- *outline the procedures for admitting and discharging a child/young person to/from your residential home;*

- *comment on an admission and a discharge that you have observed.*

Criteria for admission

The criteria for admitting children and young people to your home will largely be determined by the purpose and function of the home. You will remember from 1.1 that each home is required by the Children Act 1989 to state *what* types of services it provides for children and *how* the services will be provided.

Complete the exercise below - it will provide a useful memory aid for you to keep on file.

Record below the criteria used for admitting children/young people to your home.

Admissions

As we have said, admissions to the home will largely be determined by the purpose and function of the home. Where possible, admissions will be planned and the procedures for your home will reflect this. It is a matter of good practice to carry out some preparatory work prior to admission. For example, staff from your home may visit children and young people prior to admission and will be able to help colleagues to become familiar with their backgrounds, circumstances and needs. However, if your home provides services for children and young people in response to their personal crisis the admission procedures should reflect this.

The following tables contain a number of procedures for admitting children and young people into residential care. It is essential that the procedures are implemented carefully and as sensitively as possible as the admission can set the tone for the child/young person's stay in the home.

Tick the practices which apply to your home. Observe an admission and indicate which procedures you see.

Pre-admission	Practice	Observed date
Planning meeting to decide admission.	☐	☐
Visit by home staff to child/young person in current placement to establish links.	☐	☐
Ensure child/young person's room is clean and well equipped.	☐	☐
Key worker allocated liaises with social worker and other relevant adults.	☐	☐
Ensure that there are sufficient and appropriate staff available to support admission (key worker if possible).	☐	☐
File prepared containing all necessary paperwork.	☐	☐

	Practice	Observed date
Children and young people in home prepared for new arrival.	☐	☐
Arrangements established for child/young person's arrival and induction.	☐	☐
Staff prepared for new arrival (familiarity with background and circumstances, interests, religious, cultural, dietary needs and so on).	☐	☐
'Special needs' arrangements made.	☐	☐

The admission process may be daunting for children and young people and their families. It is important that information is kept as simple as possible. A child/young person may be so anxious that s/he retains little of what s/he is told on the day of admission. Within the first few days/weeks you must be prepared to repeat much of the information, when the child/young person needs it, in a patient and sensitive way.

Admission

	Practice	Observed date
Child/young person/social worker/parents met by home staff, preferably key worker and home manager.	☐	☐
Child/young person and accompanying adults offered refreshments.	☐	☐
Important documents collected (such as accommodation agreement, birth certification, NI number, medical card, educational documents) and filed safely.	☐	☐
Child/young person and accompanying adults reassured/questions answered by allocated staff.	☐	☐

	Practice	**Observed date**
Child/young person's belongings checked in their presence. Items inappropriate for use in the residential home stored safely or sent back with parents/social worker.	☐	
Any injuries noted and GP consulted if necessary.	☐	
Complaints procedure discussed with the child/young person and a personal copy given.	☐	
Child/young person shown to room.	☐	
Child/young person introduced to other staff and children and young people in the home.	☐	
Accompanying adults given opportunity to say farewell.	☐	
Child/young person reassured/ questions answered.	☐	
Other	☐	
Other	☐	
Other	☐	

Note: There may be some variation in the order in which the above takes place.

Discharges

While it is desirable that all children and young people leave the home in a planned manner, this is not always possible and there are rare occasions when a child/young person's placement is brought to an abrupt and unplanned end. There are procedures for both types of departure. By completing the following exercise you will be able to distinguish between the different responses required of staff in each situation.

This exercise is similar to the one that you completed in relation to admissions. Tick the procedures that apply to your home and indicate which ones you observe when a child/young person is discharged.

A *planned discharge* is one where a future placement has been identified and the staff and the child/young person are aware of the timing of the move. An *unplanned discharge* may happen if the placement is brought to an unanticipated end, such as if a young person who is remanded goes to court and is given a custodial sentence when one was not expected .

Planned discharge	**Practice**	**Observed date**
Child/young person prepared, visited future placement, if appropriate, package of post-discharge support arranged (in appropriate cases). All clothing and other possessions (including money) are checked and the child/young person or a responsible adult signs the list.	☐	
If there are discrepancies which cannot be resolved, the senior manager is informed.	☐	
The child/young person is given opportunities to say goodbye to staff and other residents.	☐	

131

	Practice	**Observed date**
Residential services manager notified of the discharge of the child/youth person.	☐	
Other	☐	

Unplanned discharge

All the child/young person's possessions including money are gathered, and checked and signed for by the representative who collects them, such as social worker, parent, relatives.	☐	
All the child/young person's possessions including money are gathered, checked and delivered by staff to their new address. Representative of young person signs for receipt of possession.	☐	
The bedroom is checked and is made ready (by staff) for the next occupant.	☐	
Residential services manager notified of the discharge of the child/young person.	☐	
Staff make contact/visit/offer support to the child/young person if appropriate.	☐	
Other	☐	

Evaluation 2.4

Objectives	Acquaintance	Familiarity	Ability to use	Relative proficiency	Competence	Date	Date	Date
Criteria for admission to the home								
Admission/ discharge procedures								
Observe an admission and a discharge								

Comments and signatures

Module 2.5 Disciplinary and control measures

Objectives

When you have completed this section you will be able to:

- *explain the purpose and application of disciplinary measures in your home;*

- *apply disciplinary procedures in a manner which provides positive learning experiences for the children and young people;*

- *identify acceptable and unacceptable disciplinary measures.*

One of your primary tasks will be to create a positive and caring ethos in the home. *The Children Act 1989 Guidance and Regulations Volume 4: Residential Care* (Department of Health, 1991b) identifies a number of indicators which encourage a positive ethos in the home. These include:

- sound management, high standards of professional practice and care planning based upon caring relationships;

- relationships between staff and children based on honesty, mutual respect and recognised good professional practice;

- an established framework of general routines and individual boundaries of behaviour that are well defined;

- children are aware of what is expected of them, what they can expect of others and how the arrangements for their care actually work;

- there is proper provision for the social, physical, emotional and intellectual needs of the children;

- there is a routine to the child's day and the correct balance is achieved between free and structured time;

- there is ample opportunity for children to participate in a range of appropriate leisure activities;

- there is consistency in the approach of all members of staff.

While such practices will help to create an environment in which children and young people can develop their personal resources, there may be occasions when they challenge the boundaries in ways which put their safety or the safety of others at risk. If this happens you may need to take disciplinary measures to maintain good order, encourage self-control and positive behaviour, and safeguard and promote the welfare of the children and young people. Such measures will only be successful if both the staff and the children and young people understand why they are necessary. It is important to discuss the need for disciplinary measures with the children and young people in a manner which they are able to understand.

Many of the children and young people in your home will have experienced significant personal difficulties and some will need help to develop their own resources and self-control. Residential care, while providing structure, must also be flexible and responsive enough to meet the individual needs of each child/young person.

The use of discipline and control measures must be consistent with the ability of the children and young people, the home's policies and the maintenance of a safe environment. The practice in your home is based on the Department of Health's *Guidance on Permissible Forms of Control in Children's Residential Care* (1993), a copy of which should be available in your home. The guidance clearly outlines the types of control measures which are effective and the situations in which they may be used.

The exercises in this section will help you to identify the measures used in your home to create and maintain good order and to safeguard and promote the welfare of all the children and young people.

Note: Your authority/agency will have a policy regarding what is acceptable and what is not acceptable as discipline and control measures. It is important that you read and understand this.

As part of their development the children and young people in your home must be able to do two things:

●   anticipate the consequences of their action;

●   make informed choices about their behaviour.

They will be helped by being given clear guidelines about what behaviour is expected of them in terms of conduct and self-control and what behaviour they can rightfully expect of others. Children and young people should be assisted in understanding what disciplinary measures may be taken as a consequence of any unacceptable behaviour from themselves and/or others.

Explaining rules and standards to children and young people

How are the rules and the expected standards of behaviour explained to the children and young people?

Consulting with children and young people - sanctions

Disciplinary and control measures may be necessary in some situations in order to safeguard children and young people from harm and to encourage more appropriate behaviour.

No one may apply measures which would deliberately harm the children and young people in any way. For this reason there are a number of measures which are **not** permitted by regulations and these are outlined in detail in *Children's Homes Regulations* (Department of Health, 1991) Volume 4, pages 17 - 19.

You may also find the table at the end of the section which gives a summary of the actions that are and are not permissible as disciplinary and control measures provides a useful checklist and point of reference.

Your home will have a range of disciplinary and control measures, often referred to as sanctions, which will be used in varying degrees depending on the age and ability of the child/young person and the nature and seriousness of his/her behaviour. You will need to become familiar with these and their application in practice in your home.

In the following exercise you are asked to consider whether the children and young people in your home have a say in agreeing the disciplinary measures and, if not, whether they should or could become involved in the process. Record also *their* views on the fairness or otherwise of the measures currently in use in the residential home.

Are the children and young people in your home involved in agreeing the disciplinary measures?

Yes ☐   No ☐

If not, should they be involved and how could you involve them?

Do they believe the sanctions used in the home are fair?

Recording disciplinary and control measures

Whenever a disciplinary measure is applied it **must** be recorded. This is a requirement of the Children Act 1989.

Where do you record disciplinary measures?

Why do you need to keep a record of disciplinary measures?

Reviewing disciplinary measures

It is important that staff in the home review the use of disciplinary measures frequently to ensure that:

- they are being applied appropriately and are not being used unnecessarily;

- they are effective in safeguarding and promoting the needs of the children and young people.

Observe current practice in your home and record your observations in the exercise that follows.

How frequently are disciplinary measures reviewed in your home?

Annually ☐

Bi-annually ☐

Quarterly ☐

Monthly ☐

Fortnightly ☐

Weekly ☐

Daily ☐

(Continued on next page.)

Are some disciplinary measures reviewed more frequently than others?

Yes ☐   No ☐

If yes, which disciplinary measures are reviewed more frequently and why?

Changing disciplinary measures

Record procedures operating in your home in the exercise below.

How are changes to disciplinary measures decided?

Are the children and young people consulted when changes are made?

How are the changes explained to the children and young people?

Case examples

On the following pages are a number of examples where it may be necessary to apply disciplinary or control measures. Explain what you would do in each case to ensure a positive learning experience for the children or young people involved and to safeguard and promote their welfare.

Case 1

Trevor tends to create a mess outside of his room and often refuses to tidy it up.

Case 2

Leonardo is 14 and persistently returns late when he goes out in the evening.

Case 3
Pauline has accused Sonia of breaking her CD. Sonia was overheard by staff the day before threatening to break it, and someone saw her do it.

Case 4
Colin (15) and Catherine (13) are fighting in the garden.

Case 5

Howard (14) repeatedly racially abuses Amir (14).

Case 6

While cleaning up after a meal Stefan, who had been agitated throughout the meal, deliberately drops a cup on your foot, leaving it sore and bruised.

Case 7

In a fit of temper Lesley repeatedly punches a wall. You ask him to stop but he appears to have lost control.

The use of discipline and control measures

Not permitted	Permitted
Corporal punishment eg slapping, pushing, punching, pinching, shaking or any 'rough' handling.	Necessary physical action to prevent injury to children and young people or staff if there is no other option. A child/young person who is out of control may be removed from the group until s/he regains control. The specific criteria for using this measure are outlined in *Guidance on Permissible Forms of Control in Children's Residential Care.*
Refusing visits, phone calls, letters as a punishment.	Contact with some individuals may be restricted as part of a care plan and after consulting the child/young person.
Depriving children and young people of food. Forcing children and young people to eat food they don't like.	Certain foods and drink may be withheld on medical advice and be recorded on the medical section of the care plan.
Depriving children and young people of sleep.	If a child/young person continually stays awake at night and sleeps in the daytime, they may be woken as part of their care plan and on medical advice to reverse the sleep pattern.
Forcing children and young people to wear distinctive clothes or clothes which are not appropriate to the activities or time of day e.g pyjamas/nighties during the daytime.	School uniform.
Using or withholding medication as punishment.	
Imposing fines. Only the courts can impose fines.	No more than two-thirds of the pocket money of a child/young person may be withheld to pay for wilful damage or theft.
Intimate physical searching.	If there are concerns about concealed weapons or drugs, the police should be notified. The child/young person's clothing may be searched following the unit's procedures.
The use of accommodation to physically restrict the liberty of any child.	Locking external doors and windows at night in line with normal domestic security. Refusing permission to go out as sanction for previous misdemeanour or if the child would be placed at risk of significant harm if they were to go out.

Evaluation 2.5

Objectives	Acquaintance	Familiarity	Ability to use	Relative proficiency	Competence	Date	Date	Date
Explain purpose of disciplinary measures								
Apply sanctions positively								
Identify acceptable measures								

Comments and signatures

Module 2.6 Working in partnership with families

Objectives

When you have completed this section you will be able to:

- *Explain the ways in which the residential home works in partnership with the families of children and young people;*

- *Identify and explain the steps taken by your residential home to promote and facilitate regular contact between children and young people and their families.*

It is both good practice and a legal requirement of the Children Act 1989 that parents, those with parental responsibility and other family members are involved in the plans for the child/young person's future, and for their day-to-day care.

The Children Act guidance makes it clear that 'measures which antagonise, alienate, undermine and marginalise parents are counter-productive'. The Guidance goes on to say that:

The development of a successful working partnership between the responsible authorities and the parents and the child, where he is of sufficient understanding, should enable the placement to proceed positively so that the child's welfare is safeguarded and promoted.

(Department of Health, Guidance and Regulations Volume 4, 1991b: 40)

Where children and young people are not in contact with their families, every effort should be made to create and maintain links with the family if this is in the best interest of the child or young person.

Contact can be maintained by personal visits from family members to the residential home or by children and young people visiting their families. Other means of maintaining contact may be used when visiting is not possible such as writing letters, telephoning or exchanging photographs.

The following exercises will help you to identify your residential home's practice in working in partnership with families, and to make suggestions for improvements to such practice.

Promoting and maintaining family contact

List below five steps taken by your home to promote and maintain contact between children/young people and their families.

1.

2.

3.

4.

5.

Did your list contain some of the following?

- Appointment of a key worker who liaises with the family.

- Copies of relevant documents relating to the child/young person sent to family.

- The home facilitates contact arrangements, such as help with travelling costs and overnight accommodation if they are necessary.

- Telephone/written correspondence encouraged and maintained.

- Liaison with social worker in relation to supporting contact.

- Offer to discuss the child/young person's progress with the family members outside of the formal review.

- Facilities which provide privacy for visits, if required.

- Family consulted about developmental, religious, cultural, education and health issues wherever possible.

- Visits home encouraged where appropriate.

Are there other steps you feel would improve parental involvement? If so how could they be facilitated? Record your suggestions below and discuss them with your supervisor

Review of contact arrangements

Review the contact arrangements of two of the children/young people in your home. How are contact arrangements planned in each case? Can anything be improved and, if so, how? You may want to think about care planning/reviews/telephone contact/written agreements/visiting arrangements/who initiates contact/timing of visits/level of staffing and so on. Any suggestions you have for improving contact should be discussed with your supervisor. You should not act on your own.

Child/young person (1)

(Continued on the next page.)

Child/young person (2)

Re-establishing contact

> **Are there any children and young people who do not have contact with their parents/family? Why is this? What, if any, steps can you or your colleagues take to help facilitate contact?**
>
> **Record your answers below, in the space provided.**
>
> **Note: Exchanges of photographs and telephone calls are often important means of remaining in touch when physical contact is not possible.**
>
> **There may be rare occasions when contact with the family may not be appropriate, and if this applies the circumstances will be recorded on the child/young person's case file. If the child is in agreement, arrangements should be made to appoint an Independent Visitor.**

Personal training

What training does your authority or agency/department provide to assist you in developing your skills for working in partnership with families?

Notifying parents about decisions which affect their child

What measures are used in your residential home to consult with parents about decisions affecting the children and young people?

Consulting with parents about decisions affecting the child/young person

How are parents notified of decisions made about their child?

Evaluation 2.6

Objectives	Acquaintance	Familiarity	Ability to use	Relative proficiency	Competence	Date	Date	Date
Promoting and maintaining family contact								
Working in partnership								

Comments and signatures

Module 2.7 Going out and coming home

Objectives

When you have completed this section you will be able to:

- *identify the home's rules on timekeeping for the children and young people;*

- *demonstrate your understanding of the procedures for responding to lateness;*

- *identify the actions you should take if a child does not return to the residential home when no arrangement for absence was made (absence without authority);*

- *identify when you should attempt to stop a child/young person from going out.*

Children and young people in residential homes will have a range of skills and abilities in keeping themselves safe. In working with this group of children and young people you need to be aware of their need for self-determination and increasing independence as well as your duty to safeguard and promote their welfare within clearly established boundaries. You will need to become familiar with the practice for the following:

- planning for going out;
- timekeeping;
- procedures if a child/young person is late;
- procedure if a child/young person does not return to the residential home when
- expected to (absence without authority);
- procedures when a child/young person returns from being absent without authority;
- procedures for preventing a child/young person leaving the home.

The children and young people should be made aware in language appropriate to their age and understanding what is expected of them and what they should expect of the staff in the circumstances listed above. The action taken by staff will be influenced by the legal status of the child or young person. There will be instances when the action you need to take will not be clear-cut. You should be given training and guidance in all the areas listed above, and opportunities to discuss the legal and practical implications of different responses. The Department of Health's training pack, *Taking Care, Taking Control* (1996), provides excellent material for facilitating team discussions in this and other related issues.

159

The following exercises will help you to clarify what actions you should take in a range of situations.

How are plans made for the children and young people's social and recreational activities?

Timekeeping

What kind of 'time-limits' are there for children and young people to return to the home?

weekdays

weekends

Are there circumstances when these can be varied? If so, what are they?

Procedures if a child/young person is late in returning home

What should a child/young person do if s/he realises that s/he will be late in returning home?

How are they enabled to do this?

What should staff do if a child/young person is late returning home?

(Continued on next page.)

Simisola is 14 and is voluntarily accommodated. She went to the cinema with her boyfriend, Shane, and was due back at 10.00 p.m. She returns at 10.45. What can you do?

What may Simisola learn from your responses?

Mohammed, age 12, was due back from school at 5.00 p.m. It is now 6.00 p.m. and he has not returned. Mohammed is the subject of a Care Order. What can you do?

What might Mohammed learn from your responses?

Procedures if a child/young person is absent without authority?

It's Monday night and Gary, aged 14, who is the subject of a Care Order rings you to say he'll be back on Wednesday evening in time for tea. He says, 'Don't worry, I'm with friends and I'm fine'. What responses can you make?

What might Gary learn from your responses?

(Continued on next page.)

Mick, aged 16, is the subject of a Care Order and is 3 hours late. He has done this before and has, in the past, returned with a full account of where he has been. What responses can you make?

What might Mick learn from your responses?

Melvin, aged 13 has been placed in the children's home under the provisions of an Emergency Protection Order as a result of physical abuse by his father. He has just telephoned to say he will be a couple of hours late back from school as he's going for a burger and milkshake with this father. He hung up before you could reply. What responses can you make?

What might Melvin learn from your responses?

(Continued on next page.)

Procedures when a child returns from an absence without authority

Lisa, aged 15, who is accommodated voluntarily, has been missing for three days. You are on shift when she returns at 10.45 p.m looking dirty and smelling of alcohol. What responses can you make?

What might Lisa learn from your responses?

Procedures for preventing a child/young person leaving the home

Peter, aged 11, is the subject of a Care Order and he has minor learning difficulties. Peter's sense of direction is poorly developed and he often gets lost. He was told he could not go to the cinema by himself but he has presented himself at the door in his coat ready to go. He is very angry because two other children are allowed to go to the cinema by themselves. What responses can you make?

What might Peter learn from your responses?

(Continued on next page.)

After a telephone call from one of his friends Dominic, aged 15, informs you that he's going out with a group of his friends and will be back in 2 hours at 10.00 p.m Dominic has been involved in stealing a car with this group of friends for which he has been charged, remanded to local authority accommodation and placed in your home. What responses can you make?

What might Dominic learn from your responses?

Evaluation 2.7

Objectives	Acquaintance	Familiarity	Ability to use	Relative proficiency	Competence	Date	Date	Date
Timekeeping								
Responding to lateness								
Absence without authority								
Attempt to stop child/young person going out								

Comments and signatures

Module 2.8 Recording and report writing

Objectives

When you have completed this section you will be able to:

- *identify what records are kept;*

- *identify the different types of recording in your residential home;*

- *identify the major purposes of recording;*

- *identify the different people for whom records are kept;*

- *demonstrate your understanding of the key issues involved in the recording of information.*

'Caring for children and young people who have been placed in a residential setting is demanding work in which staff carry great responsibility... it is work which requires high levels of professional skill. Written reports and records are an integral component of the overall professional task of caring for children and young people' (Angus Skinner, *Another Kind of Home: A Review of Residential Care* (1992)).

The records kept on each child/young person should accurately reflect every aspect of their lives. There should be detailed records relating to their health and social well being; educational progress; physical and emotional development; social interactions with other residents, staff and visitors; their contact with their families; and their progress within the residential home.

Records in residential homes are an important means of charting the development and progress of the children and young people living in them. They are also legal documents and may be required whenever decisions are being made regarding a child or young person's health, education, employment, housing, future placements or finances. Each child or young person's individual records (which must be kept for 75 years) should reflect accurately their development, progress, social interactions and their contributions to the residential home.

In addition to the detailed individual records kept on each child/young person there are also records kept on how the home is run, which will include operational information such as the staff on duty, visitors to the home, maintenance of equipment and so on. These are also very important as they provide a background against which the children and young people's development and progress can be evaluated and assessed. For these reasons all recording should be signed and dated.

The exercises in this section focus on the number, range and purpose of records kept in residential care and the individuals with legitimate access to such records. They also provide opportunities for you to comment on effective recording.

This section is informed by the work of Caroline Comben and Joyce Lishman, *Setting the Record Straight* (1995).

What records are kept?

In the exercise below, list the different records that are kept in your residential home. You may want to separate them into two lists, according to type: those which relate directly to the children and young people and those which relate to the running of your home. A few examples have been provided for each report type.

Records on children/young people	Home administration
Clothing records	Fire drills
Personal allowances/pocket money	Safety checks

Types of records - checklist

Some types of records are required to be kept by law, others are department or agency requirements, reflecting best practice.

Your lists from the previous exercise probably included a number of these examples:

- individual case files on children and young people;

- daily log book;

- complaints and compliments;

- diary (or other system of recording appointments);

- record of admissions and discharges;

- medical records including: medicines prescribed, received, administered and disposed of;

- accidents, injuries, and assaults;

- money/valuables held by staff for children and young people - including receipts;

- record of critical incidents;

- personal possessions records for children and young people;

- records of sanctions;

- rota, duty and overtime records;

- staff meeting minutes;

- care plans and reviews;

- records of visitors;

- records of achievement;

- education progress reviews;

- court reports.

Who are the records for?

You have identified a list of the kinds of records kept in your residential home, but who are you keeping these records for? Who would want to see them? Who would have a *legitimate* interest in and/or a right to see the information you record about the children and young people in your home?

Record below the people you think have a legitimate interest in the records kept in your home and any records you may write or have written.

Why do these people have a legitimate interest?

Who the records are for - a checklist

Did you include the following in the previous exercise?

- the child/young person;

- his or her parents, siblings or those with parental responsibility;

- other staff in the home;

- field social workers;

- the police;

- the courts;

- school/local education authority;

- external managers;

- trade union;

- Social Services Inspectorate;

- people involved in research;

- other professionals: GPs, psychologists, psychiatrists and so on;

- guardian ad litem;

- independent visitor;

- a child/young person's advocate;

- a child/young person's solicitor.

Access to records

Look back at the people you have listed as having an interest in your recording and complete the exercise below.

Explain how each person or group gains access to and uses the information you record.

(Further space is provided overleaf.)

Explain how each person or group gains access to and uses the information you record (cont.).

Are there any people who cannot have access to such records? Please explain your answer.

Why do we record?

List below the reasons for keeping records in homes:

You may like to compare your answers with some of those listed on the next page.

Reasons for keeping records

The following is a summary/checklist of reasons for keeping records in children's homes.

Record keeping:

- Provides information of daily progress and development of each child/young person, for example:

  - health;
  - education;
  - social.

- Provides information for use in writing reports and reviewing plans, for example:

  - care plans;
  - reviews;
  - court reports;
  - accommodation reviews.

- Provides information on the way the home is being run, for example:

  - general routines;
  - appointments;
  - use of sanctions;
  - use of restraint;
  - number of visitors;
  - accidents, injuries and action taken;
  - complaints and compliments;
  - admissions and discharges;
  - record of minutes.

All records in children's homes may be used as evidence in court. All computerised information is subject to the Data Protection Act 1984.

How do we record?

A part of your role involves recording meaningful and relevant information on the children and young people's development and progress, which facilitates planning for their immediate and longer term needs. You should be given guidance and training on how to do this in a manner which does not carry unintended judgements. Look at the following example taken from Comben and Lishman, *Setting the Record Straight* (1995), Workbook 1: 15.)

> Consider the statement 'Luke will not eat British food'. One staff team when discussing this statement at first found it factual and accurate. One member of the team, however, argued that Britain is a multicultural society and an interesting discussion followed about what the terms 'British food' meant. They then decided that it would be better to change the statement to 'Luke will not eat traditional British food'. Another team member, though, felt that from Luke's point of view, this statement may well be experienced as being oppressive, is it really saying that he is not 'one of us'? After a long discussion, they decided that they would change the statement to 'Luke will only eat the type of food which is familiar to him'. There was still some unease about this final choice. The team decided that the implications of what they write are more far-reaching than they all thought.

Remember at all times that your records should be *considered and professional*. Always try to avoid the following:

- *Ambiguity.* Is your meaning clear?

- *Jargon.* Have you used professional words and phrases which may not be understood by, say, the child/young person who may want to see what is written about him/her?

- *Racism/sexism.* Have you recorded comments which are racially or sexually derogatory or discriminating?

- *Sarcasm.* Are you having a joke at the child/young person's expense?

- *Unsubstantiated statements.* Have you provided evidence to support your opinions?

- *Stereotypes.* Have you made statements which represent a 'fixed type' of person or group?

- *Irrelevance.* Are your records relevant and meaningful?

- *Hearsay.* What is the basis of your evidence? Is it first hand or 'third party'?

Read the statements below. Think about each one and write in the left hand box whether you think the statement is 'acceptable or 'unacceptable', giving the reasons for your decision. If you are not sure, write 'don't know'.

1. Paul behaved as though he were sad: he spoke to no one, he was heard to sigh a lot and asked to go to bed early.

2. Babette was in a black mood.

3. George is really quite effeminate.

(Continued on next page.)

4.   Andy acted like a moron all night.

5.   Mary had a really good evening. She completed her homework, spoke to her mother on the phone for 15 mins and over a drink before bed, talked to me about her fears about meeting her father this weekend.

6.   Martin is a typical traveller, all charm and soft soap.

7.   Gillian indulged in her usual tomboy antics.

(Continued on next page.)

8.   Although Mark denied sniffing hair spray, I just knew he had been, though I can't prove it.

9.   Parem refused to speak to any of the staff on shift after saying he would only speak to his key worker.

10.   Greg returned from school on time and said he'd had a great day. He said he was choosen to play in the football 'A' team and was really happy about it. After tea he completed his homework and then watched TV with a broad smile for the rest of the evening.

Discuss your decisions with your supervisor.

Have you seen examples of recording in your home that you consider to be
unacceptable? What are they and why do you find them unacceptable?
What should you do in such circumstances?

Evaluation 2.8

Objectives	Acquaintance	Familiarity	Ability to use	Relative proficiency	Competence	Date	Date	Date
What records are kept								
Who records are kept for								
Purposes of recording								
Types of recording								
Key issues in recording								

Comments and signatures

march 30th

Keyworker / photocopy

(Back office)

Consultation papers

child/
parent

Soft view Sheets

reviewing / team
officer / manager

s/w

parent

Module 2.9 Care planning and reviews

Objectives

When you have completed this section you will be able to:

- *explain to a child/young person:*
  what a care plan is;
  what a review is;

- *check with a child/young person and record their understanding of:*
  why care plans are important;
  the content of a care plan;
  where reviews are held;
  who attends reviews and why;

- *help a child/young person prepare for a review;*

- *comment on the proceedings in a review.*

The care planning and reviewing process may appear complicated to new staff. It may also be confusing for the children and young people until they become familiar with the rationale and processes of review and care planning meetings. Planning for the care of children and young people in residential homes is vital if their developmental and social needs are to be met. The DOH *Looking After Children: Assessment and Action Records* (1995a) provides a comprehensive approach to the planning and monitoring process and is widely used by many local authorities and agencies.

One of your duties as a residential social worker will be to help children and young people to prepare for and participate in their care planning review meetings. This section will concentrate on working with a child/young person to ensure that s/he has as much knowledge as possible about the care planning and review procedures.

It will be useful to arrange with your supervisor to work with a child/young person in your residential home. In preparation for this you will need to read the relevant sections of your policy and procedures manual as well as the *Review of Children's Cases Regulations 1991*, a copy of which should be available in the home. You *may* need to become familiar with the procedures for completing the forms used for monitoring the children and young people's progress; these are the Department of Health (1995a) *Looking After Children: Assessment and Action Records* documents. You may also want to talk to your colleagues and other children and young people. Ruth Sinclair's book *It's your Meeting* (1995) and Carolyne Willow's *Children's Rights and Participation in Residential Care* (1996) will also be useful references.

Explaining reviews and care plans to a child/young person

In working with a child/young person, check with them their understanding of reviews and care plans. Think about the circumstances, age, understanding and ability of the child/young person together with their experience of reviews, their ethnicity, religion, language, cultural background and their health and education needs as these will influence the language you use and the issues that you need to consider.

In the following exercise, tick one box if they already know the answer and can explain it to you, tick the other if you need to explain.

Name of child/young person (initials only): ....

Age of child/young person: ....

	Already knew	**Needed explanation**
• **Does the child/young person know what a care plan is?** It is a record of: their needs and **how** these needs are going to be met, who is going to take any necessary action, by when, and when the plan will be looked at again. Do they understand their right to be consulted, to participate fully and to have their wishes and feelings heard?	☐	☐

(Continued on next page.)

	Already knew	Needed explanation

• **Does s/he know what is in a care plan?**
for example:

- name;
- date of birth;
- present address - and for how long;
- details of any court orders;
- future plans;
- family contact - frequency and duration;
- education needs;
- health needs.

☐ ☐

• **Does s/he understand the link between care plans and reviews?**

Reviews are held to reassess care plans,
to check if they are meeting his/her needs and
to change the care plan if necessary. Review
meetings are required by *Review of Children's Cases
Regulations 1991.*

☐ ☐

• **Does the child/young person know that:**

- their wishes and feelings must be taken into account?

☐ ☐

- they must be listened to?

☐ ☐

(Continued on next page.)

	Already knew	Needed explanation
Does he/she know who attends his/her review and why?		
- The child /young person so that their wishes and feelings can be taken into account.	☐	☐
- Parents and/or those with parental responsibility so that their wishes and feelings can be taken into account.	☐	☐
- Field social workers and/or their managers, who have a responsibility for helping to make the care plan work, writing reports etc.	☐	☐
- Residential social worker and/or home manager, who have day-to-day responsibility for the child/ young person, to give home's perspective.	☐	☐
- An advocate, such as: an independent visitor, guardian ad litem, Voice for the Child in Care representative. They may have something important to say on the child/young person's behalf.	☐	☐
- Other professionals, for example teachers, doctors, psychologists, psychiatrists. They may be invited occasionally if they have something to say or they may write a report which may be read in the review.	☐	☐

(Continued on next page.)

	Already knew	Needed explanation
• **Does s/he know that they can ask for someone <u>not</u> to attend their review?** Their wish will be taken into account and if possible the person/s will not be invited.	☐	☐
• **Does s/he know how often reviews must be held? that is:** - within the first four weeks of admission; - within three months after the first one; - then at no longer than at six monthly intervals; - they may be held more frequently if arrangements need to be changed.	☐	☐
• **Does s/he know where reviews are held?**	☐	☐
• **Does s/he understand the use in reviews of the information in the *Looking After Children: Assessment and Action Records* (Department of Health, 1995a)?**	☐	☐

As has been noted, the reviewing and care planning process can be confusing for children and young people and explaining it is a far from simple task for residential social workers. Some children and young people find it easier to understand such processes if they are shown graphically - (and some adults also). The planning process is shown diagramatically as being on three levels by Chris Dowis in *Statutory Reviews in Practice* (1992). This is presented as Figure 2.9.1 and may be useful in helping you to explain the process to a child or young person who does not already understand it.

Figure 2.9.1 The planning and reviewing process

Assessed needs of the child	Wishes and feelings of the child	Views of parents, wider family and network of carers
⬇	⬇	⬇

Review

Consideration of options

Arrangements   Next review

Helping a child/young person to prepare for his/her review

What is discussed in a review meeting should not come as a surprise to any of the participants. Copies of written reports will usually be made available to everyone concerned prior to the meeting. The child/young person should have an opportunity to see reports so that they can be prepared for the meeting.

You can help a child/young person to prepare for their review meeting by going through reports with them. They should, of course, have been given the opportunity to contribute to the preparation of reports by offering their opinions and explaining the situation from their perspective.

Going through reports

For the next activity, agree with your supervisor which child/young person you will work with. It is often more effective if the person who has written the report discusses it with the child/young person. If you have not written the report yourself you may want to gain permission from the person who has *or* sit in with them while they go through the report with the child/young person.

Consider the following issues when going through the report and record your observations below:

- **Which room did you use?**

- **Did it afford privacy for the child/young person?**

- **Was the report written in language that the child/young person could understand?**

- **Were explanations given for words, phrases, concepts the child/young person did not understand?**

- **Were the child/young person's wishes and feelings recorded in the report?**

- **Were issues of**
  - **ethnicity;**
  - **religion;**
  - **culture (including language);**
  - **health;**
  - **education/work;**
  - **employment;**

  addressed in the review report? Tick those which apply.

(Continued on next page.)

- **Did you listen to the child/young person?**

- **Did s/he disagree with anything in the report?**

- **How did you respond to the disagreement?**

- **How and where is the disagreement recorded?**

- **Could you have done anything else?**

(Continued on next page.)

- **If the answer is yes, what did you do to help?**

- **Other observations:**

Observing a review

The review meeting brings together the child/young person and those with responsibility for, and interest in, their welfare and development. The child/young person is central to the meeting and the way the meeting is conducted should reflect this. The following exercise requires you to observe a review and identify the participants, their roles, and how their contribution helps to safeguard and promote the welfare of the child/young person.

What type of a review meeting is it?

For each person in the review record:

1. **their name - initials only to safeguard confidentiality;**

2. **their title;**

3. **reason for attending the review;**

4. **how their contribution safeguarded and promoted the welfare of the child/young person.**

Example:

1. Ms B

2. Senior social worker

3. Attending to clarify social services' position regarding the possibility of the child/young person returning to live at home.

4. Outlined in language the child/young person could understand, the pros and cons of returning home. Spoke directly to the child/young person.

Review observation.

(Continued on next page.)

Review observation (cont.).

Evaluation 2.9

Objectives	Acquaintance	Familiarity	Ability to use	Relative proficiency	Competence	Date	Date	Date
What is a review/care plan?								
Reviews: where, who, why and content								
Help child/young person prepare for review								
Observed and commented on a review								

Comments and signatures

Module 2.10 Health

Objectives

When you have completed this module you will be able to:

identify the action taken to promote children and young people's health in your home;

state the procedures for ensuring that children and young people receive timely and appropriate health and medical care.

Health is a 'state of complete physical, mental and social well being, not merely the absence of disease or infirmity' (World Health Organisation, 1978).

Many of the children and young people in residential care have had frequent disruptions in their lives. Some have had a series of short-term placements and others have led chaotic lives with little stability and poor health care. This can lead to treatable health conditions being ignored or going undetected. Examples include hearing and sight impairment, skin complaints, and speech defects. In order to remedy such problems, 'care staff need to adopt a very vigilant attitude toward the health of children in homes. Their health should be carefully and continuously monitored and medical advice should be sought promptly when causes for concern are identified' (*The Children Act 1989 Guidance and Regulations Volume 4: Residential Care,* 1991b). In addition to helping to put things right we also have a responsibility to promote the health of each child 'with the same assiduity as would be the case for a child living with caring parents'. To ensure that this happens residential social workers should adopt a proactive approach on health issues.

The *Guidance* very clearly identifies health promotion as a duty of residential staff. You should also be aware of your duties under the United Nations' *Convention on the Rights of the Child* (1989), Article 24 and *The Health of the Young Nation* (Department of Health, 1995c).

The following exercises will help you to identify the structures already in place for promoting the health of the children and young people in your home. You should make suggestions for improvements wherever possible.

Health - promotion

This section gives an overview of the activities which should be taking place to promote the health of the children and young people in your home.

In the exercise below, tick each activity that you observe. Each time you tick the 'No' box, discuss with your supervisor and/or the manager the reasons why they are not occurring, and what you can do to help to facilitate the improvements.

	Yes	No
1. There is a clear written policy, and operational guidance on how health is promoted in the home.	☐	☐
2. Staff are familiar with *Looking after Children: Assessment and Action Records*, and children and young people's health is assessed regularly.	☐	☐
3. All staff are involved in health promotion and set good examples to the children and young people.	☐	☐
4. Health education, at a level appropriate to their ability, forms a part of all children and young people's care plans, and includes issues such as nutrition, hygiene, skin care, fitness, sleep, emotional health and dental care.	☐	☐
5. Each child/young person's care plan includes programmes of prevention of ill health and addresses issues such as immunisation, smoking, alcohol, substance misuse, sexual behaviour which may result in sexually transmitted diseases, HIV and AIDS, and mental health.	☐	☐
6. The children and young people state that their health is taken seriously and that they are being helped to grow up healthily.	☐	☐

206

Continued...   **Yes**   **No**

7. Children and young people know how and where to
    obtain information and advice on the use of contraceptives.   ☐   ☐

8. Children and young people know how and where to obtain
    information on sexual development and advice on sexual
    relationships.   ☐   ☐

9. There is a clear policy on sexual relationships between the
    children and young people.   ☐   ☐

10. Each child/young person's case records show a clear,
    complete sequence of medical and health information.   ☐   ☐

11. Staff are familiar with the health histories and needs
    of the children and young people.   ☐   ☐

12. Guidance is provided to staff on childhood ailments
    and diseases that is, how to recognise them and what
    action to take.   ☐   ☐

13. Look at the list of medical conditions in Appendix 2.
    Is training/guidance available on what action you would need
    to take in order to address these medical conditions and health
    issues?   ☐   ☐

Comments on ways to facilitate health promotion.

Health - procedures

In order to address on a practical basis the health needs of children and young people, you should be aware of the procedures in place in your home which relate to health.

---

1. **Where is the medical and health information kept?**

2. **Who has access to the children and young people's medical information? Indicate why some people have access to the information and others not. Put a tick by the side of each person with access.**

   ☐ child/young person

   ☐ medical practitioner

   ☐ dental practitioner

   ☐ parents

   ☐ home managers

   ☐ residential social workers

   (Continued on next page.)

☐   auxiliary/support staff

☐   teachers

☐   independent visitor

☐   guardian ad litem

☐   advocate/independent representative

☐   health visitor

☐   psychologist

☐   psychiatrist

☐   speech therapist

☐   optician

(Continued on next page.)

☐   police

☐   courts

☐   social workers

☐   others

☐

☐

☐

Can the children and young people refuse some individuals access to medical information?

3.   **How many GPs are involved with the children and young people in your home? What are the benefits/disadvantages (if any) of these arrangements?**

4.   **Are the children and young people satisfied with the service they receive from the GP?**

   If not, what are they dissatisfied with, and can anything be done to improve the situation?

(Continued on next page.)

5.   How are consultations with the GP arranged?

6.   Are there any special out of hours arrangements?

7. Is there a choice of a male or a female GP?

(Continued on next page.)

8. How many dental surgeons are involved with the children and young people in your home?

What are the benefits/disadvantages (if any) of these arrangements?

9. Are the children and young people satisfied with the service they receive from the dentist?

If not, what are they dissatisfied with and can anything be done to improve the situation?

(Continued on next page.)

10. **How are visits to/from the dentist arranged?**

11. **Are there any special out of hours arrangements?**

(Continued on next page.)

12. **What are the arrangements for collecting prescribed medication?**

13. **Where is medication stored?**

14. **What are the procedures for administering:**
    - **prescribed medication;**
    - **non-prescribed medication?**

(Continued on next page.)

15. At what age must children and young people's wishes about medical examination and treatment be taken into account?

16. At what age can children and young people consent to, or refuse, medical examination or treatment?

17. Who is responsible for making decisions about a child/young person in need of emergency treatment?

18. What action can be taken if a child/young person refuses life saving treatment?

Evaluation 2.12

Objectives	Acquaintance	Familiarity	Ability to use	Relative proficiency	Competence	Date	Date	Date
Identify health promotion action								
Procedures for medical care								

Comments and signatures

Module 2.11 Education

Objectives

When you have completed this section you will be able to:

- *identify the steps taken in your home to promote the education of children and young people;*

- *add suggestions for improvement, if appropriate.*

Obtaining a good education can be the key to vastly improving our chances in life. Children and young people in residential care can be particularly disadvantaged educationally. They will often have had their education disrupted as a result of changes of placements and circumstances, and may not have had the opportunity to develop to their full potential. They may have little sense of their abilities and will need encouragement to develop greater self-esteem.

A residential home can provide a stable environment from which children and young people can take full advantage of educational opportunities. It is vital that we seize this chance to promote education as valuable in itself, and as part of preparation for adulthood.

In addition to statutory provisions for education for all children and young people there are regulations and guidance specifically concerned with the education of children and young people in residential settings. These are clearly explained in the *Children Act 1989, Guidance and Regulations, Volume 4: Residential Care* (Department of Health, 1991).

The following exercises will help you to identify how education is promoted in your home and how models of good practice may be developed.

Where education is *valued* there will be a number of indicators. Work through the following list and check the indicators against the practice in your home.

'Yes' responses are indicators of good practice.

	Yes	No
1. Children and young people are reminded frequently of the benefits of education.	☐	☐
2. Staff are familiar with the educational histories and needs of the children and young people.	☐	☐
3. Each child/young person has a detailed education history and record of educational needs.	☐	☐
4. There is a clear *written* plan for addressing the educational needs of each child/young person.	☐	☐
5. Residential Social Workers are consulted when each child/young person's individual education plan is being drawn up.	☐	☐
6. Children and young people are involved in setting their own education targets.	☐	☐
7. Children and young people are encouraged to attend school or college.	☐	☐
8. Specialist tuition is provided for children and young people who do not attend mainstream school.	☐	☐
9. There are regular meetings with the schools where the children and young people are able to review their progress.	☐	☐
10. Children and young people's achievements are recognised in a manner acceptable to them.	☐	☐
11. Records of achievement show progress towards targets/goals.	☐	☐

(Continued on next page)

12 . There is an identified member of staff with
    There personal responsibility for helping each
    child/young person with out-of-school activities,
    including homework.

13. There is an identified member of staff with
     There responsibility for helping securing places
     in schools for children and young people who
     have been excluded.

14. There is an identified member of staff with
     responsibility for helping to secure out of
     school education for children and young
     people who have been excluded.

15. Parents and other significant adults are
     encouraged to take an interest in, and to
     promote, the education of the child/young
     person

16. There are appropriate places for studying and
     doing homework, for example a quiet room
     away from the main group, with desk, adequate
     lighting and pleasant decor.

17. Children/young people are encouraged to use
     local libraries.

**Score two point for each 'Yes' ticked and enter the score
in the box.**

Scores:		
28+	**=**	**Great value placed on education.**
18 - 24 points	**=**	**Education valued and an integral part of the children/young people's day.**
Less than 18 points	**=**	**Education is important but more could be done to integrate education into daily life.**

Have you observed any other activities that you consider to be good indicators of the value placed on education in your home? If so, record them below. You may find Peter Sandiford's booklet, *Improving Educational Opportunities for Looked After Young People* (1997), a useful aid to complete this exercise.

Your observations and suggestions

Have you observed anything that you consider to be unhelpful in promoting education as valuable in itself, and as part of preparation for adulthood?

What, if anything, could be done in a different way to improve practice?

Discuss with your supervisor and children and young people what your role will be in promoting the education of the children and young people.

Evaluation 2.11

Objectives	Acquaintance	Familiarity	Ability to use	Relative proficiency	Competence	Date	Date	Date
Identify steps to promote education								
Make suggestions								

Comments and signatures

Module 2.12 Comments, compliments and complaints

Objectives

When you have completed this section you will be able to:

- *identify the differences between a comment, a compliment and a complaint;*

- *demonstrate your understanding of the procedures for addressing any complaints which you may receive;*

- *demonstrate your understanding of the child/young person's right to make a complaint;*

- *identify what your rights are if you are named in a complaint.*

Children and young people in residential care are often among the most vulnerable children in society. They, and those with parental responsibility for them, rely on the services provided by residential care to ensure that their welfare is being safeguarded and promoted.

There is, built into this care arrangement, a power imbalance. The power tends to lie disproportionately with the staff in the homes and the placing authorities, it is not shared evenly with the children and young people, their families and friends.

Many recipients of social services residential care may be reluctant to complain because they fear they may lose the services or be moved. Many children and young people adopt a strategy of keeping quiet and hoping things will get better. For vulnerable children and young people this could be the baseline from which unhappiness or even abuse develops. This is perhaps the strongest reason for having a clear and *accessible* complaints and representation procedure which children and young people can use.

Comments, compliments and complaints policy and procedures

Why have a comments, compliments and complaints policy?

Such policies provide safeguards for the children and young people looked after in residential homes and they facilitate feedback from people with an interest in the home. They are a requirement of the Children Act 1989.

They form part of the checks and balances that keep abuse and oppression at bay and can prevent tensions building up. A healthy environment is one in which children and young people feel free to make complaints and where the staff use those comments to assess and if neccessary change their practice.

Purpose of representation, comments, compliments and complaints procedures

The authority/agency's representation, comments, compliments and complaints procedures aim to encourage the children and young people and their representatives to:

- tell us when they are pleased with the service we provide;

- tell us when our conduct gives them cause for concern;

- be listened to and taken seriously;

- believe that we will take steps to put things right when we realise we have got it wrong.

Defining comments, compliments, and complaints/representations

In the exercise that follows definitions of comments, compliments and complaints - as these terms are used in this manual - are given. The definitions of these terms used in your authority/agency may be different and you should record your authority/department's definition where it differs from that given here. If your authority/agency uses the term 'representation' to cover all three terms, record the definition under 'complaint'.

Your agency's definitions and those used.

Comment: 'Any expression of satisfaction or dissatisfaction about the home which does not require investigation.'

Your authority/agency's definition:

Compliment: 'Any formal expression of pleasure or satisfaction with either staff or service.'

Your authority/agency's definition:

Complaint: 'Any expression of dissatisfaction with either staff or services which requires either investigation or official response.'

Your authority/department's definition:

Representation procedures

Representation procedures can be long and complicated processes, depending on the nature of the complaint. Consult your agency's policy and consider the scenarios presented in the following exercises. Explain what action you would take, where you would record it, and what response you would expect from others involved in the representation process.

---

1. **At the meal table Gerry, who does not eat fish, complains to you that she has been given fish and chips.**

What would you do and where would you record it?

2. **Phillip tells you that he doesn't like it when you sit so close to him on the settee when you are watching the television.**

What would you do and where would you record it?

(Continued on next page.)

---

3.   Julian tells you that someone has taken his deodorant from his bedroom.

        What would you do and where would you record it?

4.   Simon tells you that he has really enjoyed the game you organised and wishes it could happen more often.

        What would you do and where would you record it?

(Continued on next page.)

5.   Babbett's mother tells you that she is really pleased with Babbette's progress and that it is all down to the care and understanding shown by the staff.

       What would you do and where would you record it?

6.   Junaid tells you that another child/young person has been constantly racially abusing him, that the staff have not sorted it out, and he wants to make a complaint.

       What would you do and where would you record it?

(Continued on next page.)

7.   Jeanette's father tells you he is not happy with the arrangements made for the observance of her religion. Jeanette is Rastafarian.

      What would you do and where would you record it?

8.   Michael's parents are concerned that his hearing impairment affects the quality of their telephone conversation when Michael rings them from the home. Michael is embarrassed by his hearing difficulties.

      What would you do and where would you record it?

(Continued on next page.)

9.   **Paul tells you that he wants to make a complaint about one of your colleagues.**

       What would you do and where would you record it?

10.   **Justine tells you that she has just made a complaint to your manager about you.**

       What would you do? What would you expect from the manager? Where would this be recorded?

You have probably indicated in your answers that where a problem arises it is usually possible to resolve the issue to the satisfaction of the complainant before a more formalised complaint is made. If the complaint proceeds to the formal stage, it will be investigated by an independent person. You will be kept informed by your manager, and/or some other nominated person, of the progress of the investigation. You will also be informed of the outcome of the complaint and investigation.

Evaluation 2.12

Objectives	Acquaintance	Familiarity	Ability to use	Relative proficiency	Competence	Date	Date	Date
Differences between comment, complaint and compliment								
Procedures for addressing complaints								
Understanding right to make complaint								
Your rights if named in complaint								

Comments and signatures

Module 2.13 Meetings

Objectives

When you have completed this section you will be able to:

●   *identify the purpose of the meetings held in your home;*

●   *chair a handover meeting;*

●   *chair other types of meetings if appropriate.*

Good residential social work is based on continuity of care. However, many children and young people in residential homes experience constant change as staff arrive for, and leave from shifts. In order to ensure continuity a handover meeting is held at the beginning of each shift. A member of staff from the departing shift will usually chair the meeting and will ensure that all relevant information is discussed with, and communicated to, the oncoming shift.

The handover meeting also provides opportunities for planning for the shift and for agreeing and maintaining consistent and coherent responses to the children and young people.

Handover meetings observations

In the exercise that follows you are required to observe three handover meetings and add a tick against the issues listed that are discussed. Space is also provided for recording other observations that you make.

	Handover 1: date	Handover 2: date	Handover 3: date
1. Behaviour of each child/young person			
2. Major incidents reported on			
3. Petty cash checked and signed for			
4. Appointments to be met/made			
5. Message book and diary discussed			
6. Staff plan activities			
7. Note senior on call			
8. Any uncompleted tasks passed to oncoming staff with reasons for non-completion			
9. A 'to do' list drawn up			
10. Manager/senior staff attends handover			
11. Handover checklist completed			

Other observations

12.			
13.			
14.			

Handover meetings chairing

In the next exercise you are required to chair three handover meetings. Your supervisor will tick the areas you discuss and add any additional feedback.

	Handover 1: date	Handover 2: date	Handover 3: date
1. Behaviour of each child/young person			
2. Major incidents reported on			
3. Petty cash checked and signed for			
4. Appointments to be met/made			
5. Message book and diary discussed			
6. Staff plan activities			
7. Note senior on call			
8. Any uncompleted tasks passed to oncoming staff with reasons for non-completion			
9. A 'to do' list drawn up			
10. Home manager/senior staff attends handover			
11. Handover checklist completed			

Additional feedback

12.			
13.			
15.			

Comments and signatures

Other types of meeting and their purposes

Throughout the course of a day, a week, a month or a year there will be a variety of meetings. They will each have a specific function which will be reflected by the people who attend and the issues that are discussed. You will be involved in some meetings quite regularly and in others less frequently. It will be useful to identify each meeting and its purpose so that you are clear about what is required of yourself and others. These meetings do not include reviews which are dealt with separately in section 2.9.

In the exercises that follow, identify all the routine meetings which take place at regular intervals and any that occur less frequently. For each meeting record the type of meeting, the purpose it serves and who attends.

Daily meetings

Meeting: . . . .

Purpose: . . . .

Who attends: . . . .

. . . .

. . . .

Meeting: . . . .

Purpose: . . . .

Who attends: . . . .

. . . .

. . . .

Meeting: . . . .

Purpose: . . . .

Who attends: . . . .

. . . .

. . . .

Weekly meetings

Meeting: . . . .

Purpose: . . . .

Who attends: . . . .

. . . .

. . . .

Meeting: . . . .

Purpose: . . . .

Who attends: . . . .

. . . .

. . . .

Meeting: . . . .

Purpose: . . . .

Who attends: . . . .

. . . .

. . . .

Monthly meetings

Meeting: . . . .

Purpose: . . . .

Who attends: . . . .

. . . .

. . . .

Meeting: . . . .

Purpose: . . . .

Who attends: . . . .

. . . .

. . . .

Meeting: . . . .

Purpose: . . . .

Who attends: . . . .

. . . .

. . . .

Quarterly meetings

Meeting: ....

Purpose: ....

Who attends: ....

....

....

Meeting: ....

Purpose: ....

Who attends: ....

....

....

Meeting: ....

Purpose: ....

Who attends: ....

....

....

Meetings occurring less frequently

Meeting: ....

Purpose: ....

Who attends: ....

....

....

Meeting: ....

Purpose: ....

Who attends: ....

....

....

Meeting: ....

Purpose: ....

Who attends: ....

....

....

Chairing meetings

If, as a residential social worker, you are expected to chair any of the meetings you have listed, identify which meetings you chaired and ask your supervisor to sign and comment on three of these meetings.

Meeting	Date chaired	Signed
. . . .		
. . . .		
. . . .		

Comments and signatures

Evaluation 2.13

Objectives	Acquaintance	Familiarity	Ability to use	Relative proficiency	Competence	Date	Date	Date
Identify the purpose of various meetings								
Chair handover meetings								
Chair other meetings								

Comments and signatures

Module 2.14 Moving On

Objectives

When you have completed this section you will be able to:

* *identify the ways that your residential home helps young people to prepare for leaving care.*

When children and young people cease to be looked after they will return to live with their families, live with substitute families or live independently.

Leaving residential care can be a significant 'milestone' for a young person irrespective of the length of time they have lived in the home. The quality of the relationships formed and the way that the young person is prepared for the transition from residential care to independence will influence the young person's future.

The Children Act; sections 21, 61 and 64 make it clear that the preparations for a young person leaving care must begin well in advance of the time that a young person ceases to be looked after.

Preparation for the process of leaving care should be incorporated into the care plan of a young person as soon as s/he starts to be looked after. Residential homes 'play a leading role in preparing young people for the time when they leave care' (Department of Health Guidance and Regulations Volume 4 1991: 105) Other agencies such as schools and the Careers Service, health authorities and housing departments should also be involved and the residential staff should be working closely with these agencies to secure the best outcomes for the young people.

Volume 4 of the Department of Health Guidance and Regulations also identifies three broad issues to be taken into account when preparing young people for leaving care. These are:

* enabling young people to build and maintain relationships with others (both general and sexual relationships);
* enabling young people to develop their self-esteem;
* teaching practical and financial skills.

The guidance states:

> The capacity to form satisfying relationships and achieve interdependence with others is crucial to the future well-being of the young person. With such a capacity, he is much more likely to cope with the transition to adulthood and the special difficulties associated with leaving care. It is crucial, therefore, that the experience of being cared for provides both the opportunity for such personal development and attention that is required when special help is needed. Many young people who are being, or have been cared for, have described feelings of shame about being cared for. It is therefore all the more necessary to encourage young people from the day they begin to be cared for, to value themselves; to regard their experience of being cared for without embarrassment; and to be able to explain calmly to other people why they are being cared for and how they feel about it.

> (Department of Health, 1991:105)

The following exercises will help you to identify indicators of good practice for preparing young people for leaving care and to explain the practice in your residential home.

Building and maintaining relationships

Describe the ways in which young people are helped to build and maintain relationships, including sexual relationships where appropriate.

Developing self-esteem

Describe how children and young people are helped to develop their self-esteem.

Practical and financial skills and knowledge

Describe the opportunities available for young people to develop practical and financial skills in the following areas:

• **Food and diet:**
      - shopping for, preparing and cooking food;
      - eating a balanced diet.

(Continued on next page.)

• **Laundry, sewing and other housekeeping skills.**

• **Safety in the home and first aid.**

(Continued on next page.)

• **The cost of living and budgeting.**

• **Health education, including personal hygiene.**

• **Sex education, including contraception and preparing for parenthood.**

(Continued on next page.)

- **Applying for a course of education and training.**

- **Applying for and being interviewed for a job.**

- **The rights and responsibilities of being an employee.**

(Continued on next page.)

• **Applying for social security benefits.**

• **Applying for housing and locating and maintaining it.**

(Continued on next page.)

• **Registering with a doctor and a dentist.**

• **Knowledge of emergency services (fire, police, ambulance).**

• **Finding and using community services and resources.**

(Continued on next page.)

• **Contacting the social services department and other welfare agencies.**

•**Contacting organisations and groups set up to help young people.**

• **The role of agencies such as the Citizens Advice Bureau, local counsellors and MPs.**

• **How to write a letter (a) of complaint (b) to obtain advice.**

(Continued on next page.)

Use this space to record other effective practices you observe which are not included and/or make suggestions for introducing additional practices. You may find James Cathcart's book, *Preparation for Adulthood* (1997), useful.

Evaluation 2.14

Objectives	Acquaintance	Familiarity	Ability to use	Relative proficiency	Competence	Date	Date	Date
Preparing children/ young people for leaving care								

Comments and signatures

References

Access to Personal Files Act 1987. HMSO

Access to Personal Files (Social Services) Regulations 1989. HMSO

Cathcart, J (1997) *Preparation for Adulthood.* National Children's Bureau

Children Act 1989. HMSO

Comben, C and Lishman, J (1995) *Setting the Record Straight.* HMSO

The Declaration on Primary Health Care at Alma Ata 1978. World Health Organisation

Department of Health (1991a) *The Children Act 1989 Guidance and Regulations Volume 1: Court Orders.* HMSO

Department of Health (1991b) *The Children Act 1989 Guidance and Regulations Volume 4: Residential Care.* HMSO

Department of Health (1991c) *Children's Homes Regulations.* HMSO

Department of Health (1993) *Guidance on Permissible Forms of Control in Children's Residential Care.* HMSO

Department of Health (1994) *Standards for Residential Child Care Services.* HMSO

Department of Health (1995a) *Looking After Children: Assessment and Action Records.* HMSO

Department of Health (1995b) *Looking After Children: Good Parenting, Good Outcomes.* HMSO

Department of Health (1995c) *The Health of the Young Nation.* HMSO

Department of Health (1997) *Taking Care, Taking Control.* HMSO

Department of Health (1996) *The Control of Children in the Public Care: Interpretation of the Children Act 1989.* HMSO

Dowis, C (1992) *Statutory Reviews in Practice.* British Association of Adoption and Fostering *Food Safety Act 1990.* HMSO

Health and Safety at Work Act 1974. HMSO

Kahan, B (1994) *Growing Up in Groups.* NISW/HMSO

Sandiford, P (1997) *Improving Educational Opportunities for Looked After Young People.* National Children's Bureau

Sinclair, R (1995) *It's Your Meeting.* National Children's Bureau

Skinner, A (1992) *Another Kind of Home: A Review of Residential Care.* HMSO

Statutory Instrument No.895 Children and Young Persons *Review of Children's Cases Regulations 1991.* HMSO

Statutory Instrument No. 1505 Children and Young Persons *Children's Home Regulations 1991.* HMSO

The United Nations General Assembly (1989) *The Convention on the Rights of the Child.* UNICEF

Willow, C (1996) *Children's Rights and Participation in Residential Care* National Children's Bureau

World Health Organisation (1978) *The Declaration on Primary Health at Alma Ata.* World Health Organisation

Module 3

Introduction to Module 3

Aim

To consolidate your knowledge and understanding of the purpose of residential child care within the broader context of children's services, and to help you to develop an awareness of the specific roles and responsibilities of other child-care professionals and agencies.

Module content

3.1   Roles and responsibilities of child care professionals, agencies and the courts

Completion

In order to complete Module 3 effectively you will need to:

- liaise with a number of professionals from within and outside your home and employing authority/agency;

- arrange and make a series of observational and information gathering visits within the child care system;

- consult your local authority's children's services plan.

You will need to plan your visits carefully in order to complete this module. Your visits should be discussed with your supervisor and preparations should be made at the earliest opportunity to carry them out.

Module 3.1 Roles and responsibilities of child care professionals, agencies and the courts

Objectives

• *When you have completed this section you will be able to:*

• *Explain the specific roles and responsibilities of different professionals and agencies in relation to their work with children and young people.*

• *Compare the purpose, function and operation of your own home with other residential homes in the child care system;*

• *Explain the court processes which provide for the placement of children and young people in residential care.*

There is a wide range of statutory and voluntary agencies who have an interest in, and an impact upon, the lives of children and young people in residential care. Their representatives are working toward the best outcome for the children and young people. Some, such as the independent visitor or a child protection manager, should be working directly on behalf of the child/young person. Others, such as the training officer and equal opportunities officer, may have no regular direct contact with the children and young people, and will appear to be working on behalf of the staff. However, by helping staff to fulfil their potential an improved quality of service should also be delivered to the children and young people.

By completing the following exercises you will be able to demonstrate your understanding of the responsibility to the child/young person that each role carries. It will be useful to discuss the role and responsibilities of the various professionals with the postholders.

For each professional role or agency highlighted in the following exercises, record the specific role and responsibilities they carry, in the space provided. In addition, record how these individuals/agencies safeguard and promote the welfare of children/young people living in residential care.

Role of the children and families team

What is the role of the children and families team?

How can the children and families team safeguard and promote the welfare of children and young people living in residential care?

Role of the family placement team

What is the role of the family placement team?

How can the family placement team safeguard and promote the welfare of the children and young people in residential care?

Role of the youth justice team

What is the role of the youth justice team?

How can the youth justice team safeguard and promote the welfare of children and young people in residential care?

Role of the child protection team

What is the role of the child protection team?

How can the child protection team safeguard and promote the welfare of children and young people in residential care?

Role of the children's rights officer

What is the role of the children's rights officer?

How can the children's rights officer safeguard and promote the welfare of children and young people living in residential care?

Role of the independent visitor

What is the role of the independent visitor?

How can the independent visitor safeguard and promote the welfare of children and young people in residential care?

Role of the guardian ad litem

What is the role of the guardian ad litem?

How can the guardian ad litem safeguard and promote the welfare of children and young people in residential care?

Role of the external line manager

What is the role of the external line manager?

How can the external line manager safeguard and promote the welfare of children and young people in residential care?

Role of children's services manager

What is the role of the children's services manager?

How can the children's services manager safeguard and promote the welfare of children and young people in residential care?

Role of the Social Services Inspectorate

What is the role of the Local Authority Registration and Inspection Unit?

How can the Local Authority Registration and Inspection Unit safeguard and promote the welfare of children and young people in residential care?

Role of the equal opportunities officer

What is the role of the equal opportunities officer?

How can the equal opportunities officer safeguard and promote the welfare of children and young people in residential care?

Role of the training officer

What is the role of the training officer?

How can the training officer safeguard and promote the welfare of children and young people in residential care?

Role of other services

Are there any further agencies and professional services which may safeguard and promote the welfare of children and young people in residential care?

If so, what are they and how can they safeguard and promote the welfare of children and young people?

Role of other residential homes and courts

The following exercises provide opportunities for you to demonstrate your knowledge and understanding of the legal processes experienced by the children and young people and the different placements they may have experienced, or may experience in the future.

By visiting other residential homes and the courts further opportunities are created for sharing best practice, and for developing an understanding of the broader context of child care and youth justice.

Visits to other homes

Arrange to visit other homes.

Compare the other homes visited with your own, paying particular attention to:

- **purpose and function;**
- **legal status of children and young people;**
- **staff qualification and experience;**
- **education/training of children and young people;**
- **employment of children and young people;**
- **daily routines;**
- **management structure;**
- **recreation activities;**
- **children and young people's perspectives and views;**
- **the physical structure.**

Visit to the family proceedings court

Arrange a visit to a family proceedings court at a time agreed with your supervisor/manager.

Observe and record the proceedings, paying particular attention to:

- the names/titles of main participants;
- the process (including the child/young person's role in the proceedings);
- the style of address to the bench;
- the layout of the court;
- the attire of the participants;
- your feelings.

(Continued on next page.)

What is the primary jurisdiction of the family proceedings court?

(Continued on the next page.)

In what circumstances would a child/young person need to attend a family proceedings court?

How is a family proceedings court staffed? List the professionals involved.

(Continued on next page.)

How can you use your knowledge and understanding of the family proceedings court in your work with children and young people?

Visit to a youth court

Arrange to visit a youth court at a time agreed with your supervisor/manager.

Observe and record the proceedings, noting in particular:

- **names/titles of main participants;**
- **the process (including the child/young person's role in the proceedings);**
- **style of address;**
- **the layout of the court;**
- **the attire of the participants;**
- **your feelings.**

(Continued on next page.)

What is the primary jurisdiction of the youth court?

(Continued on next page.)

In what circumstances might a child/young person need to attend a youth court?

How is the youth court staffed? List the professionals involved.

(Continued on next page.)

How can you use your knowledge and understanding of the youth court in your work with children and young people?

Visit to a High Court

Arrange a visit to a High Court at a time agreed with your supervisor/manager

Observe and record the proceedings, noting in particular;

- **names/titles of main participants**
- **the process (including the child/young persons role in the proceedings**
- **style of address**
- **the layout of the court**
- **the attire of the participants**
- **your feelings**

(Continued on next page.)

What is the primary jurisdiction of a High Court?

(Continued on next page.)

In what circumstances might a child/young person attend a High Court?

How is the High Court staffed? List the professionals involved

(Continued on next page.)

How can you use your knowledge and understanding of the High Court in your work with children and young people?

Evaluation 3.1

Objectives	Acquaintance	Familiarity	Ability to use	Relative proficiency	Competence	Date	Date	Date
Roles and responsibilities of various professionals and agencies to children and young people								
Comparison of home with other facilities								
Court processes and jurisdiction								

Comments and suggestions

Appendix 1 Residential child care: an introduction to the legal framework

Best residential social work practice is informed by knowledge and a familiarity with the relevant law, guidance and regulations.

What follows is an introduction to the principal legal provisions that impact upon residential social work practice. This introduction is not exhaustive but it will guide you through the key elements of law in relation to your work.

Further readings are suggested at the end of this appendix.

Law, guidance and regulations: some definitions

The principal piece of legislation (law) in relation to residential and field social work with children, young people and their families is the Children Act 1989. The status of the Children Act, as with other Acts of Parliament, is generally understood: it is the *law* and as such it must be observed. However, in addition to the Act itself there are also several volumes of *regulations and guidance*. With regard to residential social work with children and young people perhaps the most commonly used is *The Children Act 1989 Guidance and Regulations Volume 4: Residential Care* (refer to *'Further reading'* at the end of this appendix). Although this is very important and you will probably refer to it regularly, people tend to be less clear about the status of *regulations and guidance* than they are about the *law*.

Regulations and guidance are sometimes also referred to as *subordinate legislation,* as they are made under the authority of an Act which is the *primary legislation*. Regulations, however, also have the full force of the Act. In other words, they are equally important to all areas of social work practice: 'they include permissions and restrictions as to what may or may not be done and also requirements on what must be done' (Department of Health, 1990: 2).

Guidance documents, as the very term suggests, are issued as general guidance which is intended to be a statement of what is held to be good practice. Though guidance is not technically law it should none the less be followed, as it will be included in local authority policy and practice papers including the Statement of Purpose and Function which applies to the children's home where you work. Guidance and regulations are often issued together in the some document, as is the case with Volume 4 referred to above.

The Children Act 1989

The Children Act received Royal Assent in November 1989 and come into force in October 1991. The Act is a comprehensive piece of legislation about children, young people and their families and it forms the basis of the modern law relating to their care and welfare. The Children Act lies at the foundation of both residential social work and field social work.

Some key principles of the Children Act 1989

There are a number of key principles and concepts that lie at the heart of the Act:

• *The welfare principle and the welfare checklist*

Section 1(1) of the Children Act 1989 provides that:

> When a court determines any question with respect to
> (a) the upbringing of a child; or
> (b) the administration of the child's property or the application of any income
> arising from it, the child's *welfare* shall be the court's *paramount* consideration.
> (Our italics.)

The key terms here are 'welfare' and 'paramount' and as such, this is sometimes referred to as the 'paramountcy principle'. The welfare or paramountcy principle means that the court is required to take full account of the promotion of the child's welfare and her/his best interests before reaching its decision.

Section 1(3) of the Act provides a checklist to guide the court which shall have regard in particular to:

    (a)   the ascertainable wishes and feelings of the child concerned (considered in the light of his age and understanding);

    (b)   his physical, emotional and educational needs;

    (c)   the likely effect on him of any change in his circumstances;

    (d)   his age, sex, background and any characteristics of his which the court considers relevant;

    (e)   any harm which he has suffered or is at risk of suffering;

    (f)   how capable each of his parents, and any other person in relation to whom the court considers the question to be relevant, is of meeting his needs;

    (g)   the range of powers available to the court under this Act in the proceedings in question.

- *The no-delay principle*

Section 1(2) of the Children Act 1989 reminds us that any undue delay in court in reaching decisions regarding the upbringing of children and young people is likely to be harmful to them. The Act and its associated guidance and regulations stresses that delay is to be avoided.

- *The minimumy intervention principle or the no-order principle*

The minimum intervention principle or the no-order principle is, according to Freeman, 'the key to an understanding of the whole Act' (1992: 17). In practical terms this means that the court should not make a child the subject of a statutory order (a Care Order, for example) unless it considers that to do so 'would be better for the child than making no order at all' (Section I (5)). This principle rests upon the established finding that children and young people are generally best looked after within their own families. Even when a period living away from home is necessary, the minimum intervention principle or the no-order principle provides that this should (whenever possible) be arranged voluntarily, in full cooperation with parents and in such a way as to maintain family contact (refer to the *'partnership principle'* below and *'Duties to children "looked after" in residential care'* and *'Agreements and Planning'*.)

- *The partnership principle*

Although the actual word 'partnership' is not mentioned in the Act the spirit of partnership runs through all of its provisions and features prominently within the associated guidance and regulations:

> The development of a working partnership with parents is usually the most effective route to providing supplementary or substitute care for their children. Measures which antagonise, alienate, undermine or marginalise parents are counter-productive.
>
> (Department of Health, 1990: 8)

It follows therefore that best residential social work practice involves:

1.   Working in partnership with parents.

2.   Establishing clearly defined voluntary agreements collaboratively (wherever practicable).

3.   Taking full account of the wishes and feelings of children and young people.

4.   Facilitating contact arrangements of children, young people and their families.

297

Children in need

Part 111 of the Children Act 1989 - *Local Authority Support for Children and Families* - largely defines the duties of a local authority to 'children in need'. According to section 17(10) of the

Act a child is 'in need' if:

(a)   he is unlikely to achieve or maintain, or to have the opportunity of achieving or maintaining, a reasonable standard of health or development without the provision for him of services by a local authority under this Part;

(b)   his health or development is likely to be significantly impaired, or further impaired, without the provision for him of such services; or

(c)   he is disabled.

Furthermore, Section 17(11) of the Act defines *development* as 'physical, intellectual, emotional, social or behavioural development', and *health* as 'physical or mental health'.

A child or young person is regarded as *disabled* under this section of the Act if she/he is 'blind, deaf or dumb or suffers from mental disorder of any kind or is substantially and permanently handicapped by illness, injury or congenital deformity or such other disability as may be prescribed'.

Services for children in need

Where a child has been recognised as being 'in need', a local authority has a general duty under the provisions of the Children Act 1989 to safeguard and promote their welfare, and (so far as it is consistent with that general duty) to promote their upbringing by their family by providing a range and level of services appropriate to their need.

Schedule 2 of the Act outlines the services that can be made available to 'children in need', and the powers of local authorities to provide a range of inter-agency services; financial assistance; day care and/or supervised activities; family centres and associated services.

In providing services to 'children in need' local authorities should always consider their appropriateness in accordance with the religious persuasion, racial origin and cultural and linguistic background of the child (refer to *'Duties to children "Looked After" in residential care'.*)

In cases where it is not possible to promote the upbringing of 'children in need' by their family, the local authority has a range of legal duties to provide other forms of accommodation including residential care.

Children and young people 'looked after' in residential care

Where a child or young person is provided with accommodation (a residential placement or a family placement) under the provisions of the Children Act 1989, they are regarded as being 'looked after' by the local authority. 'Looked after' is a generic term which can apply equally to children and young people who are being accommodated *voluntarily* (as a result of an agreement between the local authority and their parents and/or others with parental responsibility), and those who are being accommodated as a result of a *court order* or under the *direction of the court or police* (see below).

In relation to residential care, therefore, children and young people may enter the children's home under different legal provisions and via different routes or pathways. Essentially, there are four such legal pathways into residential care:

• *The 'child in need' pathway*

This pathway is provided by Section 20(1) of the Children Act 1989, which places a duty on a local authority to provide accommodation for a 'child in need' in any of four circumstances:

1.   There is no person who has parental responsibility for them.

2.   They are lost or abandoned.

3.   The person who ordinarily cares for them has been prevented (temporarily or permanently) from providing suitable accommodation or care.

4.   They have reached the age of 16 and the authority considers that without the provision of accommodation their welfare is likely to be seriously prejudiced.

• *The 'safeguarding or promoting welfare' pathway*

This pathway is provided by Section 20(4) and Section 20(5) of the Children Act 1989 which places duties on a local authority to provide accommodation for a child or young person in either of two circumstances:

1. Even though they have a person with parental responsibility for them who is able to provide accommodation the local authority feels that it is necessary to provide alternative accommodation in order to safeguard and promote their welfare.

2. They are between the ages of 16 and 21 and the local authority feels that it is necessary to provide accommodation to safeguard and promote their welfare.

Note: Children and young people who are 'looked after' under the provisions of Section 20 of the Children Act 1989 (that is those who have entered accommodation by either the 'child in need' or the 'safeguarding or promoting welfare' pathway) are provided with accommodation on a voluntary basis.

While the local authority is under a duty, or is empowered, to provide accommodation in these circumstances, it does not acquire parental responsibility in so doing. The local authority only acquires parental responsibility if the child is the subject of a statutory court order (see below).

- *The 'Care Order' pathway*

This pathway is provided by Section 31 of the Children Act 1989 which enables the court to make a Care Order on the application of a local authority. Under a Care Order a local authority acquires parental responsibility, for the child or young person. Although the local authority is vested with parental responsibility however, the parents remain the parents and as such they retain parental responsibility although they are not entitled to act in any way which is incompatible with the Care Order.

Section 31(2) of the Act provides that the court will only make a care order if it is satisfied that:

- (a)   that the child concerned is suffering, or is likely to suffer, significant harm; and
- (b)   that the harm, or likelihood of harm, is attributable to:
    - (i)   the care given to the child, or likely to be given to him if the order were not made, not being what it would be reasonable to expect a parent to give to him; or
    - (ii)   the child being beyond parental control.

In making its decision the court is required to take into account the four principles that we considered earlier (refer to 'Some Key Principles of the Children Act' above).

- *The 'police or court direction' pathway*

This pathway is provided by Section 21 of the Children Act 1989 which requires local authorities to provide accommodation for children and young people in particular and specified circumstances. There are essentially four legal categories within which such children and young people fall:

1.   Section 21(1) of the Act which relates to children and young people who have either been removed from home or kept away from home under Emergency Protection Orders

or Child Assessment Orders.

2.   Section 21(2)(a) of the Act which relates to children and young people who have been taken into police protection.

3.   Section 21(1)(b) of the Act which relates to children and young people who have been arrested and detained.

4.   Section 21(2)(c) of the Act which relates to children and young people who have been remanded into local authority accommodation or required to reside in local authority accommodation as a condition of a court order.

It is very important to remember that although children and young people may enter residential care (together with other forms of accommodation) via different legal pathways, they all share common needs and have a right to good quality care when they are being 'looked after'. The Children Act places duties on local authorities which must be observed in the provision of care for all children and young people who are 'looked after'.

Note: With specific regard to residential child care the above legal pathways apply to children and young people who enter 'open' community homes and residential provision. For an outline of the legal pathways that apply to secure accommodation refer to Goldson (1995); Gabbidon and Goldson (1997); and Gabbidon (1998).

Duties to children 'looked after' in residential care

The Children Act 1989 places duties on local authorities which must be observed in providing residential services for children and young people:

• *The duty to safeguard and promote welfare*

Section 22(3) of the Act provides that any accommodation provided by the local authority should be consistent with the child's or young person's welfare and should be part of a plan for the child or young person:

It shall be the duty of a local authority looking after a child:
(a) to safeguard and promote his welfare.

• *The duty to consult and take account of wishes and feelings*

Sections 22(4) and Section 22(5) of the Act provide that the local authority must consult with, and seek the wishes and feelings of, relevant people before making any decision with respect to a child or young person who they are looking after or proposing to look after. Section 22(4) of the Act states:

a local authority shall, so far as is reasonably practicable, ascertain the wishes and feelings of:

        (a) the child;

        (b) his parents;

        (c) any person who is not a parent of his but who has parental responsibility for him; and

        (d) any other person whose wishes and feelings the authority consider to be relevant.

Section 22(5) of the Act requires the local authority to give 'due consideration' to the wishes and feelings of such people in making any decision in relation to the child or young person.

• *The duty to take account of religion, race, culture and language*

Section 22(5)(c) of the Act requires local authorities to give 'due consideration' to the child's or young person's 'religious persuasion, racial origin and cultural and linguistic background'. This provision must be understood and applied in conjunction with the principles that underpin the relevant regulations and guidance. The Department of Health notes:

> Since discrimination of all kinds is an everyday reality in many children's lives, every effort must be made to ensure that agency services and practices do not reflect or reinforce it ... Ethnic minority children should be helped to be proud of their racial and cultural heritage. Those of minority religions need opportunities to understand, value and practice their faith.
>
> (Department of Health, 1990: 11)

Agreements and planning

The importance of agreements and clear care plans cannot be over-stated in relation to ensuring best residential child care practice and making sure that the duties outlined above are observed and applied. Agreements and plans also provide excellent opportunities for working in partnership as we discussed earlier (refer to 'Some key principles of the Children Act 1989').

Agreements should involve the child or young person, those with parental responsibility, other relevant people and representatives from Social Services. The plan for the implementation of the arrangements made under the agreement will set out (among other things):

1.   The reasons for the child's or young person's stay in local authority accommodation.

2.   The purpose of and anticipated length of stay in local authority accommodation.

3.   The contact arrangements.

The advantages of agreements and planning include:

1.   The expectations, roles and responsibilities of all concerned are clear.

2.   The child or young person's views are recognised as are those of her/his parents.

3.   Progress can be carefully measured and reviewed

4.   The key issues can be identified and addressed.

5.   Accountability can be ensured.

After-care

Good residential care involves helping children and young people to prepare for adulthood and the time when they will no longer be 'looked after' by a local authority. Moreover, Section 24(1) of the Children Act 1989 places a duty on local authorities to assist children and young people with such preparation:

> Where a child is being looked after by a local authority, it shall be the duty of the authority to advise, assist and befriend him with a view to promoting his welfare when he ceases to be looked after by them.

Young people also qualify for advice and assistance once they cease to be 'looked after' or 'leave care'. Section 24(2) of the Act defines 'a person qualifying for advice and assistance' as:

> a person within the area of the authority who is under twenty-one and who was, at any time after reaching the age of sixteen but while still a child:
> (a)   looked after by a local authority;
> (b)   accommodated by or on behalf of a voluntary organisation;
> (c)   accommodated in a registered children's home;
> (d)   accommodated:
>   (i)   by any health authority or local education authority; or
>   (ii)   in any residential care home, nursing home or mental nursing home for a consecutive period of at least three months; or
> (e)   privately fostered but who is no longer so looked after, accommodated or fostered.

Representations and complaints

The establishment of clearly defined procedures for dealing with representations and complaints is an important feature of best residential social work practice. Section 26(3) of the Children Act 1989 requires local authorities to establish such procedures and Section 26(8) of the Act requires that the procedures are properly explained and publicised.

Section 26(3) provides that representations and complaints can be made to a local authority by:

(a) any child who is being looked after by them or who is not being looked after by them but is in need;

(b) a parent of his;

(c) any person who is not a parent of his but who has parental responsibility for him;

(d) any local authority foster parent;

(e) such other person as the authority consider has a sufficient interest in the child's welfare to warrant his representations being considered by them.

Section 26(4) of the Act provides that the system for investigating representations and complaints must include an independent element.

Further reading

The purpose of this appendix is to provide an *introduction* to the legal framework within which residential social work with children and young people is located. It is imperative that residential social workers have a reasonable grasp of law, guidance and regulations if they are to provide the best service for children and young people who are 'looked after'. You will develop a knowledge of the legal framework by using this manual, through your direct practice and by means of additional training. You may also find the following references useful and the texts marked with * are particularly recommended:

Cathcart, J (1997) *Preparation for Adulthood: Standards for Good Practice in Residential Care.* National Children's Bureau

*Department of Health (1989) *An Introduction to the Children Act.* HMSO

*Department of Health (1990) *The Care of Children: Principles and Practice in Regulations and Guidance.* HMSO

Department of Health (1991) *The Children Act 1989 Guidance and Regulations Volume 1: Court Orders.* HMSO

Department of Health (1991) *The Children Act 1989 Guidance and Regulations Volume 2: Family Support, Day Care and Educational Provision for Young Children.* HMSO

*Department of Health (1991) *The Children Act 1989 Guidance and Regulations Volume 4: Residential Care.* HMSO

Department of Health (1991) *The Children Act 1989 Guidance and Regulations Volume 5: Independent Schools.* HMSO

Department of Health (1991) *The Children Act 1989 Guidance and Regulations Volume 6: Children with Disabilities.* HMSO

Department of Health (1991) *The Children Act 1989 Guidance and Regulations Volume 7: Guardians ad Litem and other Court Related Issues.* HMSO

Department of Health (1991) *The Children Act 1989 Guidance and Regulations Volume 8: Private Fostering and Miscellaneous.* HMSO

Department of Health (1991) *The Children Act 1989 Guidance and Regulations Volume 9: Adoption Issues.* HMSO

Department of Health (1991) *The Children Act 1989 Guidance and Regulations Volume 10: Index.* HMSO

*Department of Health (1991) *Working Together under the Children Act 1989: A Guide to Arrangements for Inter-Agency Co-operation and for the Protection of Children from Abuse.* HMSO

Eekelaar, J and Dingwall, R (1990) *The Reform of Child Care Law: A Practical Guide to the Children Act 1989.* Routledge

Freeman, M (1992) *Children, their Families and the Law: Working with the Children Act.* Macmillan

*Gabbidon, P and Goldson, B (1997) *Securing Best Practice: An Induction Manual for Residential Staff Working in Secure Accommodation.* National Children's Bureau

*Grimshaw, R and Sinclair, R (1997) *Planning to Care: Regulation, Procedure and Practice Under the Children Act 1989.* National Children's Bureau

*Macdonald, S (1992) *All Equal Under the Act?* NISW Race Equality Unit

References

Department of Health (1990) *The Care of Children: Principles and Practice in Regulations and Guidance.* HMSO

Freeman, M (1992) *Children, their Families and the Law: Working with the Children Act.* Macmillan

Gabbidon, P (1998) *Taking Liberty.* National Children's Bureau

Gabbidon, P and Goldson, B (1997) *Securing Best Practice.* National Children's Bureau

Goldson, B (1995) *A Sense of Security.* National Children's Bureau

Kahan, B (1994) *Growing Up in Groups.* HMSO

SSI (1994) *How Well Are Children Being Looked After?* Department of Health

Appendix 2 Health issues

Are you aware of the action you need to take in order to address the following medical conditions and health issues?

Tick whichever applies. You may wish to add notes and/or references to relevant information sources or documents.

Health issues	No knowledge of	Some knowledge of	Good knowledge of

Child and adolescent development			
Growth, puberty and sexual development Cognitive, social and emotional development			

Health promotion programme			
Immunisation Growth monitoring Hearing and sight screening Health education Sex education			

Health issues	No knowledge of	Some knowledge of	Good knowledge of
Common childhood ailments and conditions			
Coughs Colds Sore throat Conjunctivitis Earache Headache Stomach ache Head lice Bedwetting Soiling			

Adolescent health issues			
Self-esteem and identity Acne and spots Sexuality Fatigue Nutrition and diet Eating problems Personal hygiene Anaemia Body piercing			

Mental health			
Mood changes Anxiety Stress Depression Loss, bereavement and grief Self-harm and suicide			

Health issues	No knowledge of	Some knowledge of	Good knowledge of
Sexual health			
Sex education Relationships Contraception Sexually transmitted diseases Pregnancy Abortion			
Drugs and other substance misuse			
Alcohol Solvents Tobacco Prescribed drugs Over-the-counter drugs Illegal drugs			
Skin conditions			
Impetigo Dandruff Warts Verrucas Spots and acne Boils and rashes Psoriasis Athletes foot Eczema Sunburn			

Health issues	No knowledge of	Some knowledge of	Good knowledge of
Accidents and emergencies			
Cuts, wounds and bleeding Falls Fractures Poisoning Burns and scalds Choking Fainting Respiratory arrest Cardiac arrest			
Chronic disease and disabilities			
Asthma Diabetes Epilepsy Sickle cell anaemia Thalassaemia Migraine Hearing and visual disabilities Arthritis			